FAMILY FINANCE
WORKBOOK

DISCOVERING THE BLESSINGS
OF FINANCIAL FREEDOM

FRANK DAMAZIO
&
RICH BROTT

CITYBIBLE
PUBLISHING

Published by City Bible Publishing
9200 NE Fremont
Portland, Oregon 97220

Printed in U.S.A.

City Bible Publishing is a ministry of City Bible Church, and is dedicated to serving the local church and its leaders through the production and distribution of quality materials. It is our prayer that these materials, proven in the context of the local church, will equip leaders in exalting the Lord and extending His kingdom.

For a free catalog of additional resources from City Bible Publishing please call 1-800-777-6057.

ABOUT THE AUTHORS

FRANK DAMAZIO

Frank Damazio and his Australian-born wife, Sharon, have four children and live in Portland, Oregon. After graduating from Portland Bible College in 1976, he taught full-time at PBC until 1981. He then pioneered a successful church in Eugene, Oregon, until 1992. Returning to Portland, he succeeded Pastor Dick Iverson as senior pastor of City Bible Church in October of 1995.

City Bible Church is a large and influential 4000 member church in the city of Portland. Pastor Frank Damazio leads the City Pastor's Network in city prayer and intercession, citywide racial reconciliation and city leadership.

Along with his Bachelor of Theology degree, Pastor Frank also holds a Master of Divinity degree from Oral Roberts University. He is currently president of Portland Bible College and vice-chairman of Ministers Fellowship International, a fellowship of several hundred ministers and missionaries. He has authored several books*: The Making of a Leader, Developing the Prophetic Ministry, Effective Keys to Successful Leadership, The Vanguard Leader, Seasons of Revival, Seasons of Intercession, From Barrenness to Fruitfulness, Crossing Rivers and Taking Cities, The Gate Church, The Power of Spiritual Alignment*, and his most recent work, *Miracles: Receiving the Miracles Prepared for You.*

RICHARD A. BROTT

Rich Brott holds a Bachelor of Science degree in Business and Economics and a Master of Business Administration.

Rich has served as CEO of some very successful businesses. He has functioned on the board of directors for churches, businesses, charities and served on advisory boards for colleges. Formerly the Family Life pastor at City Bible Church, Rich currently serves as the director of City Bible Publishing.

He has authored four books, including his most recent CBP bestseller titled *the Family Finance Handbook*. He and his wife, Karen, have been married for 33 years. The Rich Brott family has three children: Julie, Jana and Nathaniel and son-in-law Ollie White.

FAMILY FINANCE
WORKBOOK

DISCOVERING THE BLESSINGS
OF FINANCIAL FREEDOM

*E*verything we have belongs to God—including our finances. He owns our finances; we manage them. How can we know how to effectively manage them? God does not expect us to bear this responsibility alone. Isn't this encouraging? We have the counsel of the Holy Spirit as well as biblically based principles that we need to apply in our daily financial lives. We have also been blessed with books like the Family Finance Workbook written by Frank Damazio and Rich Brott, anointed pastors and experienced businessmen, who have provided this financial road map to help keep us on course.

Dear reader, the financial strength of the Christian home is the basis for the financial strength of the local church. If individuals and families will manage their personal finances according to godly principles, then the ministry of the local church can also advance on a biblical foundation as God intended. Living according to God's values and principles will make us successful.

I pray that our Heavenly Father will abundantly bless your family with financial health through the reading of the Family Finance Workbook, so that you may also bless others for His glory.

DR. DAVID YONGGI CHO, SENIOR PASTOR
YOIDO FULL GOSPEL CHURCH
SEOUL, KOREA

LESSON CONTENTS

—MODULE 1—
GOD'S ECONOMY

1 Money in God's Economy 15
2 The Cycle of Money 29
3 The Blessing of Giving 39

—MODULE 2—
MAN'S STEWARDSHIP

4 Principles of a Blessed Person 51
5 Persona of a Steward 61
6 Disciplines of a Steward 73

—MODULE 3—
FAMILY DECISIONS

7 How to Make Wise Family Decisions 83
8 Facing Financial Challenges 91
9 Defining Your Financial Future 97

—MODULE 4—
SPENDING MANAGEMENT

10 Managing Your Cash Flow 109
11 Financial Benefits of Budgeting 117
12 Designing That Perfect Budget 125
13 Developing the Savings Habit 135
14 Borrowing and Credit Issues 143

—MODULE 5—
MAKING LIFESTYLE CHANGES

15 Getting Out of Debt 153
16 Making Lifestyle Changes 165
17 Areas of Financial Vulnerability 177

—MODULE 6—
INVESTING WITH A VISION

18 Investing for Your Future 185
19 Planning for Retirement 195
20 Preparing for the Unexpected 205

Answer Key 211

INTRODUCTION

1. **This Course Is about Lifestyle**

   a. Living According to Certain Biblical Principles

   b. Enjoying God's Blessing

   c. Living in Peace with Yourself and Your Family

2. **Understanding the Bigger Picture**

   a. Your Attitude toward Life

   b. Your Understanding of God's Purpose

   c. Your Lifestyle of Christian Stewardship

3. **Stewardship**

   a. It involves every area of our being.

   b. Exercising good personal discipline every day will help me even in difficult circumstances.

   c. Practical resource and financial management are second to Biblical principles.

   d. Stewardship is allowing the Lord to direct our lives; this produces the Biblical "abundant and prosperous life".

4. **Problems**

   a. Problems, financial and otherwise, are common to all people.

   b. Problems should be faced with a calm and confident attitude, knowing that God's resources are available, and that He cares for us.
   "And even the very hairs of your head are all numbered." (Matthew 10:30)

5. **Temptation to Indulge in Short-Term Pleasure**

   a. Self-discipline is necessary when faced with temptation that will cause you to stray from financial goals and personal vision.

   b. Temptation is not the cause of trouble or wrong-doing, but our choices determine right or wrong action.

   c. Set goals and establish definite steps to reach them.

6. **Family Dynamics**

   a. Clear communication between spouses concerning finance is necessary.

   b. Parents must be an example of wise financial stewards.

   c. Be flexible and admit when mistakes have happened.

7. **Money**

   a. What we are is more important than what we possess.

   b. Our handling of money should reflect God's interest in what He has entrusted to us.

8. **Principles Addressed in This Course**

   a. Time that is planned and invested wisely will bring future benefit.

   b. Honesty, integrity and accountability are more important than wealth.

   c. Getting out of debt and investing for the future require attitude before action.

   d. Spending management is necessary for future success.

   e. We live in this world, but we seek a heavenly reward.

   "Do not store up for yourselves treasures on earth, where moth and rust destroy, and where thieves break in and steal. But store up for yourselves treasures in heaven, where moth and rust do not destroy, and where thieves do not break in and steal. For where your treasure is, there your heart will be also." (Matthew 6:19-21)

NOTES

Module 1

GOD'S ECONOMY

Lesson One

MONEY IN
GOD'S ECONOMY

"In his heart a man plans his course, but the LORD determines his steps."
PROVERBS 16:9

"Make all you can, save all you can, give all you can."
JOHN WESLEY

"Money never made a man happy yet, nor will it. There is nothing in its nature to produce happiness. The more a man has, the more he wants. Instead of filling a vacuum, it makes one."
BENJAMIN FRANKLIN

Lesson One

MONEY IN GOD'S ECONOMY

1. **Introduction**

   a. Ordering your life according to God's values and _____ will make you successful.

   b. A value system built on dishonesty, lying, cheating and stealing leads to disaster.

2. **Success in God's Economy**

   Those who live according to God's principles can _____ the wealth and treasure awaiting them in heaven, which outweighs the temporal wealth of this world.

❧

If our possessions belong to God, nothing is powerful enough to take them away.

---

3. **Material Possessions**

   a. Contentment must be a _____ value.

   b. When we have abundance, our lives are not to be caught up in our possessions.

   "Then he said to them, 'Watch out! Be on your guard against all kinds of greed; a man's life does not consist in the abundance of his possessions.'" (Luke 12:15)

   c. The Lord is our _____ and substance.

"But godliness with contentment is great gain. For we brought nothing into the world, and we can take nothing out of it. But if we have food and clothing, we will be content with that. People who want to get rich fall into temptation and a trap and into many foolish and harmful desires that plunge men into ruin and destruction.

For the love of money is a root of all kinds of evil. Some people, eager for money, have wandered from the faith and pierced themselves with many griefs. But you, man of God, flee from all this, and pursue righteousness, godliness, faith, love, endurance and gentleness."

(I Timothy 6:6-11)

4. **Real Contentment**

   a. Money cannot buy _____ or happiness.

   b. People find happiness in proportion to the degree that they give.

   c. Those who are "in Christ" have the _____ to be content.

   d. Recognize your treasures: the love of family and friends, etc.

5. **The Love of Money**

   "Once when we were going to the place of prayer, we were met by a slave girl who had a spirit by which she predicted the future. She earned a great deal of money for her owners by fortune-telling...

   She kept this up for many days. Finally Paul became so troubled that he turned around and said to the spirit, 'In the name of Jesus Christ I command you to come out of her!' At that moment the spirit left her.

   When the owners of the slave girl realized that their hope of making money was gone, they seized Paul and Silas and dragged them into the marketplace to face the authorities...

   The crowd joined in the attack against Paul and Silas, and the magistrates ordered them to be stripped and beaten. After they had been severely flogged, they were thrown into prison, and the jailer was commanded to guard them carefully. Upon receiving such orders, he put them in the inner cell and fastened their feet in the stocks." (Acts 16:16,18,19,22-24)

a. The love of money causes _____ to others.

b. The love of money values possessions over people.

c. The love of money gets rich off of _____ weakness.

6. **What I Am, Not What I Possess**

a. God places importance on the methods used to make money.

"Fools mock at making amends for sin, but goodwill is found among the upright." (Proverbs 14:9)

"The house of the righteous contains great treasure, but the income of the wicked brings them trouble." (Proverbs 15:6)

b. Shedding all sense of _____ for the sake of money is foolish.

c. God rewards faithfulness and enables greater ministry through generosity.

"... 'Well done, good and faithful servant! You have been faithful with a few things; I will put you in charge of many things. Come and share your master's happiness.'" (Matthew 25:21)

"You will be enriched in everything for all liberality." (II Corinthians 9:11)

7. **Lack of Contentment**

a. Don't allow what you don't have to _____ you of the joy of gratefulness.

"You shall not covet your neighbor's house. You shall not covet your neighbor's wife, or his manservant or maidservant, his ox or donkey, or anything that belongs to your neighbor." (Exodus 20:17)

b. Resist the world's view that claims we have to have things to be happy.

c. Discontentment can cause us to toss aside _____ and integrity.

Acts 5:1-10, Matthew 26:14,15; Matthew 27:5

d. We have to make a choice to serve God or money.

8. The Price of Greed

a. Over-commitment to _____ can cause failure.
    Samuel 15:3,9, 26

b. When the desire for money becomes an obsession, nothing can satisfy.

c. Greedy people may have everything, but they don't have a _____ heart and a clear conscience.

9. Living without Distractions

a. Don't be _____ with creating great gain.

"So do not worry, saying, 'What shall we eat?' or 'What shall we drink?' or 'What shall we wear?' For the pagans run after all these things and your heavenly Father knows that you need them. But seek first His kingdom and His righteousness, and all these things will be given to you as well. Therefore do not worry about tomorrow, for tomorrow will worry about itself. Each day has enough trouble of its own." (Matthew 6:31-33)

"I am not saying this because I am in need, for I have learned to be content whatever the circumstances. I know what it is to be in need, and I know what it is to have plenty. I have learned the secret of being content in any and every situation, whether well fed or hungry, whether living in plenty or in want." (Philippians 4:11,12)

Money is a tool, not a treasure.

b. Be thankful and don't worry about every little thing.

   c. Use money as a _____ , not a means to accumulate material goods.

   d. Not money, but spiritual treasures accumulated on earth will pass with us to eternity.

   e. Knowing Christ is to be _____ wealthy.

10. Values and Principles

   a. Our walk in God's economic world is faith-based.

Ordering your life according to His values and principles will make you successful by any measurement.

---

   b. God takes _____ in our lives for our ultimate benefit.

   c. As stewards, we are required to give a faithful account for what God has entrusted to us.

11. Our Natural Economy

Naturally, we experience debt, bankruptcy, recession, depression and other financial crises, but in God's _____ , these do not exist.

12. God's Supernatural Provision

   a. God turns _____ into much.
Matthew 14:19-21

   b. The level of our blessing may depend on the level of our faith.
II Kings 4:1-7

In God's economy there is no such thing as want, lack, recession or depression.

13. Wealthy People of the Bible

a. There is no harm in _____ riches. (Joseph of Arimathea, Barnabas, Abraham, Solomon)

b. Harm comes when _____ possess us.

"Now listen, you rich people, weep and wail because of the misery that is coming upon you. Your wealth has rotted, and moths have eaten your clothes. Your gold and silver are corroded. Their corrosion will testify against you and eat your flesh like fire. You have hoarded wealth in the last days. Look! The wages you failed to pay the workmen who mowed your fields are crying out against you. The cries of the harvesters have reached the ears of the Lord Almighty. You have lived on earth in luxury and self-indulgence. You have fattened yourselves in the day of slaughter." (James 5:1-3)

c. Wealth is short-lived.

"Do not store up for yourselves treasures on earth, where moth and rust destroy, and where thieves break in and steal. But store up for yourselves treasures in heaven, where moth and rust do not destroy, and where thieves do not break in and steal. For where your treasure is, there your heart will be also." (Matthew 6:19-21)

14. The Stewardship of Possessions

"But godliness with contentment is great gain. For we brought nothing into the world, and we can take nothing out of it. But if we have food and clothing, we will be content with that. People who want to get rich fall

into temptation and a trap and into many foolish and harmful desires that plunge men into ruin and destruction. For the love of money is a root of all kinds of evil. Some people, eager for money, have wandered from the faith and pierced themselves with many griefs." (I Timothy 6:6-10)

a. The stewardship of material _____ comes to grips with the question of ownership.

"Whoever can be trusted with very little can also be trusted with much, and whoever is dishonest with very little will also be dishonest with much. So if you have not been trustworthy in handling worldly wealth, who will trust you with true riches? And if you have not been trustworthy with someone else's property, who will give you property of your own? No servant can serve two masters. Either he will hate the one and love the other, or he will be devoted to the one and despise the other. You cannot serve both God and Money." (Luke 16:11-13)

b. What we care about we _____ in. *II Corinthians 8:4-7*

Be a conduit, not a dam. It is not about what we have, but what has us.

---

c. Stewardship means recognizing your obligation to God because of Calvary.

15. Our Position as Trustee

a. Placing _____ First

"But seek first his kingdom and his righteousness, and all these things will be given to you as well." (Matthew 6:33)

b. Trusting God's Provision

c. God's _____ to Bless

"Delight yourself in the LORD and he will give you the desires of your heart." (Psalms 37:4)

16. Responsible with Finances

a. God is the _____ so we must be responsible.
Deuteronomy 8:18

b. Our time on earth is short and then we go to an eternal destination.
"But store up for yourselves treasures in heaven, where moth and rust do not destroy, and where thieves do not break in and steal. For where your treasure is, there your heart will be also." (Matthew 6:20,21)

c. Cherish _____ treasure.

NOTES

STUDENT RESPONSE

Improvement Action Plan

What I need to change: _____

What? I define my goal as this achievable result. What will be my final outcome?

My answer: _____

_____

Why? This is why I need to accomplish my goal.

My answer: _____

_____

Who? Who will be involved in making me successful?

My answer: _____

_____

Where? Where will I get started? In what area will I begin?

My answer: _____

_____

How? How will I accomplish what I want to achieve? How will I measure my progress?

My answer: _____

_____

When? When will I begin working on achieving this goal?

My answer: _____

_____

Lesson Two

THE CYCLE
OF MONEY

"All streams flow into the sea, yet the sea is never full. To the place the streams come from, there they return again."
ECCLESIASTES 1:7

"Then God said, 'Let the land produce vegetation; seed-bearing plants and trees on the land that bear fruit with seed in it, according to their various kinds.'"
GENESIS 1:11

"Make money your God, and it will plague you like the devil."
HENRY FIELDING (1707–1754)

"Fame is a vapor, popularity is an accident, money takes wings, those who cheer you today may curse you tomorrow. The only thing that endures is character."
HORACE GREELEY

Lesson Two

The Cycle of Money

1. **The Cycle of Nature**

   a. The Seed Cycle

   b. The _____ Cycle

       i)   Precipitation can become useful groundwater.

       ii)   Precipitation can also be stored.

2. **The Cycle of Money**

   a. When _____ comes our way, we should use it for our needs and for the good of others.

   b. The measure we give determines the measure we receive.

   "Give, and it shall be given you; good measure, pressed down, and shaken together, and running over, shall men give into your bosom. For with the same measure that ye mete withal it shall be measured to you again." (Luke 6:38, KJV)

   c. God multiplies and _____ the resources of the giver.

   II Corinthians 9:6-15

3. **The Significance of Giving**

Giving money is significant to God because giving money is a way to give of yourself.

"Lay not up for yourselves treasures upon earth, where moth and rust doth corrupt, and where thieves break through and steal: But lay up for yourselves treasures in heaven, where neither moth nor rust doth corrupt,

and where thieves do not break through nor steal: For where your treasure is, there will your heart be also." (Matthew 6:19-21, KJV)

a. The wealthy have an _____ to the needy.

b. Unused wealth will get you nowhere.

   "Your wealth has rotted, and moths have eaten your clothes. Your gold and silver are corroded. Their corrosion will testify against you." (James 5:2,3a)

c. All _____ can be destroyed.

The Law of living is giving. If money is to be useful, it must be used.

---

4. **The Law of Sowing and Reaping**

   a. The seed we _____ is the same kind we will reap: seed of its kind.

   b. We determine the size of the harvest at the time of planting.

      II Corinthians 9:6,8,11

   c. We will _____ have a harvest.

      Malachi 3:10, Galatians 6:9

   d. You usually reap later than you sow.

   e. We always _____ more than we plant.

      Matthew 13:8

   f. There is a season for planting and a season for harvesting.

      Ecclesiastes 3:1,2

   g. Seed can be sown secretly, but the _____ will be viewed by many.

   h. We are responsible to sow, but God is responsible for bringing the harvest.

5. Principles of Personal Finance

a. God _____ everything.

    i) Understanding this puts you in a position to prosper as you partner with God.

        "The earth is the Lord's, and everything in it, the world, and all who live in it." (Psalms 24:1)

        "'The silver is mine and the gold is mine,' declares the LORD Almighty." (Haggai 2:8)

        "For every animal of the forest is mine, and the cattle on a thousand hills. I know every bird in the mountains, and the creatures of the field are mine." (Psalms 50:10,11)

    ii) God gives you the ability to earn a living.

b. How _____ Is Obtained

    i) The manner in which finances are acquired and disbursed must be based on sound moral guidelines.

If God cannot trust you with $100 now, how can He trust you with $1,000 or $100,000?

---

    ii) With access to resources comes _____ – you must prove yourself a good steward.

    iii) Our life's stewardship should reflect God's interest in all that He has trusted us with.

        Genesis 1:26, 2:15

    iv) The value system of one's heart is _____ by one's relationship to money and material things.

        Matthew 19:16-22

    v) Spend your time investing in things of eternal nature.

vi)   Those who "have everything", but not a loving family, a clean heart, honor, and the _____ of God are miserable.

Money and possessions, at best, only last a lifetime. At worst, they don't last at all.

---

vii)   Leaving all scruples and morals for the sake of money is foolish.

viii)   God is concerned about our _____ and motives.

c.   How Money Is Disbursed

i)   Not money, but our attitude about it may be wrong.

"People who want to get rich fall into temptation and a trap and into many foolish and harmful desires…" (I Timothy 6:9)

ii)   We will be blessed if we use the monetary blessings God has given us to finance His cause and _____ His kingdom.

"For we brought nothing into this world, and it is certain we can carry nothing out." (I Timothy 6:7)

"For in him we live and move and have our being." (Deuteronomy 8:18)

"But remember the LORD your God, for it is He who gives you the ability to produce wealth…" (Acts 17:28)

"For every living soul belongs to me." (Ezekiel 18:4)

"Therefore, I urge you, brothers, in view of God's mercy, to offer your bodies as living sacrifices, holy and pleasing to God." (Romans 12:1)

"Know that the LORD is God. It is he who made us, and we are his; we are his people, the sheep of his pasture." (Psalms 100:3)

"You are not your own; you were bought at a price. Therefore honor God with your body." (I Corinthians 6:19-20)

iii)   Don't try to figure out how little you can give; give God _____ and ask how much you should keep.

d.   How Money Is Contributed

i)   Your use of money must not violate the laws of the land or the principles of God's Word.

In business, when you partner with God, He not only will bless it, He will let you enjoy prosperity.

---

ii)   Our motives and _____ must reflect, "God first, me last."

"Seek ye first the kingdom of God, and his righteousness; and all these things shall be added unto you." (Matthew 6:33)

iii)   Though ungodly men and women achieve prosperity apart from God, they can never achieve the deep, settled peace that comes from God.

Psalms 73:3, Proverbs 13:22

iv)   Giving is the _____ for financial miracles.

Luke 6:38, II Corinthians 9:6

NOTES

STUDENT RESPONSE

Improvement Action Plan

What I need to change: _____

What? I define my goal as this achievable result. What will be my final outcome?

My answer: _____

_____

Why? This is why I need to accomplish my goal.

My answer: _____

_____

Who? Who will be involved in making me successful?

My answer: _____

_____

Where? Where will I get started? In what area will I begin?

My answer: _____

_____

How? How will I accomplish what I want to achieve? How will I measure my progress?

My answer: _____

_____

When? When will I begin working on achieving this goal?

My answer: _____

_____

Lesson Three

THE BLESSING
OF GIVING

"But just as you excel in everything – in faith, in speech, in knowledge, in complete earnestness and in your love for us – see that you also excel in this grace of giving."
II CORINTHIANS 8:7

"... remembering the words the Lord Jesus himself said: 'It is more blessed to give than to receive.'"
ACTS 20:35

"Give, and it will be given to you. A good measure, pressed down, shaken together and running over, will be poured into your lap. For with the measure you use, it will be measured to you."
LUKE 6:38

"Never measure generosity by what you give, but by what you have left."
FULTON SHEEN

"When it comes to giving until it hurts, most people have a very low threshold of pain."
ANONYMOUS

"Never worry about numbers. Help one person at a time, and always start with the person nearest you."
MOTHER TERESA

Lesson Three

THE BLESSING OF GIVING

1. **God's Perspective**

   Our wealth does not come from what we grab in life, but from what we
   _____ in life.

2. **A Blessing or a Curse**

   James 5:1-3

There is no harm in possessing riches as long as the riches do not possess you.

---

3. **Ultimate Ownership**

   You own _____ and God owns everything.

4. **A God-Given Ability**

   God gives you the _____ to earn.

   "But remember the LORD your God, for it is he who gives you the ability to produce wealth..." (Deuteronomy 8:18)

   "The earth is the LORD's, and everything in it, the world, and all who live in it." (Psalms 24:1)

   "For every animal of the forest is mine, and the cattle on a thousand hills. I know every bird in the mountains, and the creatures of the field are mine." (Psalms 50:10,11)

   "Know that the LORD is God. It is he who made us, and we are his; we are his people, the sheep of his pasture." (Psalms 100:3)

"For every living soul belongs to me." (Ezekiel 18:4)

"'The silver is mine and the gold is mine,' declares the LORD Almighty."
(Haggai 2:8)

"For in him we live and move and have our being." (Acts 17:28)

"Therefore, I urge you, brothers, in view of God's mercy, to offer your
bodies as living sacrifices, holy and pleasing to God." (Romans 12:1)

5. **We Are Not Our Own**

Because you _____ to God, all you have belongs to Him.

"You are not your own; you were bought at a price. Therefore honor God
with your body." (I Corinthians 6:19-20)

6. **The Joy of Giving**

When God is our _____, our well will not run dry and we will
be able to.

Nothing happens in the economy of God until you give something away.

"Will a man rob God? Yet you rob me. But you ask, 'How do we rob
you?' In tithes and offerings. You are under a curse— the whole nation of
you— because you are robbing me. Bring the whole tithe into the
storehouse, that there may be food in my house. Test me in this," says the
LORD Almighty, "and see if I will not throw open the floodgates of
heaven and pour out so much blessing that you will not have room
enough for it. I will prevent pests from devouring your crops..."
(Malachi 3:8-11)

"One man gives freely, yet grows all the richer; another withholds what he should give, and only suffers want. A liberal man will be enriched, and one who waters will himself be watered." (Proverbs 11:24, RSV)

"Don't be deceived, my dear brothers. Every good and perfect gift is from above, coming down from the Father..." (James 1:16,17)

7. **Our Only Resource**

    God is the source of your _____ supply.

    "And my God shall supply all your need according to His riches..." (Philippians 4:19, NKJ)

8. **Be Careful about Greed**

    Spiritual prosperity is more _____ than material prosperity.

    "Watch out! Be on your guard against all kinds of greed; a man's life does not consist in the abundance of his possessions." (Luke 12:15)

    "Beloved, I pray that you may prosper in all things and be in health, just as your soul prospers." (III John 2, NKJ)

    "As long as [King Uzziah] sought the LORD, God gave him success." (II Chronicles 26:5)

    "Do not let this Book of the Law depart from your mouth; meditate on it day and night, so that you may be careful to do everything written in it. Then you will be prosperous and successful." (Joshua 1:8)

9. **The Blessing of Tithing**

    a. God is training us to be faithful _____ in handling money.

People who do not pay a tithe, or tenth, of their income often have poor financial habits that leave them broke soon after payday.

---

b. Tithing is commanded.

"Bring ye all the tithes into the storehouse." (Malachi 3:10)

"Let every one of you lay by him in store, as God hath prospered him." (I Corinthians 16:2)

c. Abraham _____ before the law of Moses.

Genesis 14:11-20

d. The New Testament recounts the first tithe.

Hebrews 7:1-19

e. A _____ is a tenth.

10. First Fruits

Tithing does away with "hit and miss" methods of giving.

11. Jesus Christ Endorsed Tithing.

Luke 18:22

Jesus Himself _____; we know this because only tithers were allowed into the homes of Pharisees.

Luke 11:37

12. Jesus Christ Approved the Tenth.

Matthew 23:23, Matthew 22:21

13. Solomon Taught Tithing.

"Honour the LORD with thy substance, and with the firstfruits of all thine increase: So shall thy barns be filled with plenty, and thy presses shall burst out with new wine." (Proverbs 3:9-10, KJV)

The only way to get our treasures into heaven is to put them into something that is going to heaven.

14. Beyond the Tithe

Giving is _____ and God will see that we reap a harvest.

"Be not deceived; God is not mocked: for whatsoever a man soweth, that shall he also reap." (Galatians 6:7, KJV)

"Bring ye all the tithes into the storehouse, that there may be meat in mine house, and prove me now herewith, saith the LORD of hosts, if I will not open you the windows of heaven, and pour you out a blessing, that there shall not be room enough to receive it." (Malachi 3:10)

15. Giving Expresses Our Love.

"Each man should give what he has decided in his heart to give, not reluctantly or under compulsion, for God loves a cheerful giver." (II Corinthians 9:7)

"If I give all I possess to the poor and surrender my body to the flames, but have not love, I gain nothing." (I Corinthians 13:3)

16. Giving Freely

A giving person gives with a spirit of genuine _____. When he or she receives, it is a totally unexpected blessing.

"Good will come to him who is generous.... He has scattered abroad his gifts to the poor, his righteousness endures forever; his horn will be lifted high in honor." (Psalms 112:5,9)

"...without expecting to get anything back. Then your reward will be great..." (Luke 6:35)

"It is more blessed to give than to receive." (Acts 20:35, KJV)

Freely giving protects us from the pitfalls of greed and materialism.

17. Giving and Obedience

Generous giving comes from a humble and loving heart.

18. Bountiful Giving

When you give, give bountifully and generously with pure motives.

N O T E S

S T U D E N T   R E S P O N S E

Improvement Action Plan

What I need to change: _____

What? I define my goal as this achievable result. What will be my final outcome?

My answer: _____

_____

Why? This is why I need to accomplish my goal.

My answer: _____

_____

Who? Who will be involved in making me successful?

My answer: _____

_____

Where? Where will I get started? In what area will I begin?

My answer: _____

_____

How? How will I accomplish what I want to achieve? How will I measure my progress?

My answer: _____

_____

When? When will I begin working on achieving this goal?

My answer: _____

_____

49

Lesson Four

PRINCIPLES OF A
BLESSED PERSON

"The LORD will open the heavens, the storehouse of His bounty, to send rain on your land in season and to bless all the work of your hands. You will lend to many nations but will borrow from none."
DEUTERONOMY 28:12

"If a person gets his attitude towards money straight, it will help straighten out almost every other area of his life. Tell me what you think about money and I can tell you what you think about God for these two are closely related. A man's heart is closer to his wallet than almost anything else."
BILLY GRAHAM

"I am a little pencil in the hand of a writing God who is sending a love letter to the world."
MOTHER TERESA

Lesson Four

PRINCIPLES OF A BLESSED PERSON

1. The Heart Attitude

The blessed person gives of his or her resources freely, _____, and out of genuine appreciation to God.

Generosity is God's antidote to greed.

---

2. Money Cannot Buy Happiness.

"Then he said to them, 'Watch out! Be on your guard against all kinds of greed; a man's life does not consist in the abundance of his possessions.'" (Luke 12:15)

3. Principles of Blessing

* The principle of knowing that God _____ it all *(Haggai 2:8-9, I Corinthians 4:2, Psalms 50:10, II Corinthians 9:7)*

* The principle of giving from the top *(Genesis 14:20, Proverbs 3:9)*

* The principle of supernatural provision *(I Kings 17:14-16)*

Are we a conduit, or do we stop the stream of God's favor?

---

* The principle of being _____ *(Matthew 17:27, Ecclesiastes 9:11, Hebrews 12:1,2, Proverbs 21:5)*

- The principle of knowing how to be content *(I Timothy 6:8-9)*

- The principle of resisting world views *(Romans 12:2)*

We must resist the world's view of wealth, happiness and possessions. We do not have to have it all!

- The principle of _____ left over *(II Corinthians 9:8-9)*

- The principle of feeding the local house *(Malachi 3:10)*

- The principle of obedience *(Malachi 3:10)*

- The principle of _____ preparation *(Genesis 41:47-49)*

- The principle of honesty *(Malachi 3:8,10, Matthew 6:33)*

- The principle of _____ possessions *(I Timothy 6:7-8)*

- The principle of giving to the needy *(I John 3:17)*

- The principle of right attitudes *(II Corinthians 9:6-9)*

- The principle of _____ giving *(I Corinthians 16:2-3)*

- The principle of giving freely *(Matthew 10:8)*

- The principle of never withholding *(Proverbs 11:24-28, I Kings 17)*

- The principle of the tenth *(Genesis 28:20-22)*

Giving starts with tithing.

- The principle of increased measure *(Luke 6:38)*

- The principle of _____ prosperity *(Joshua 1:8-9)*

- The principle of supply *(Philippians 4:18-20)*

- The principle of _____ giving *(Mark 12:41-44)*

- The principle of heart decisions *(II Corinthians 9:7)*

- The principle of equal giving *(II Corinthians 8:10-12)*

- The principle of _____ *(I Corinthians 4:2-3, Deuteronomy 5:32)*

Stewardship is the management of our entire life, all that we have and all that we are.

- The principle of laying up treasures *(I Timothy 6:19)*

- The principle of the sluggard lifestyle *(Proverbs 24:30-34, Proverbs 12:27)*

- The principle of _____ diligently *(Proverbs 6:6-11, Proverbs 22:29)*

- The principle of brotherhood *(I John 3:17, Romans 12:13)*

- The principle of giving out of your poverty *(II Corinthians 8:1-5)*

- The principle of giving gifts *(II Corinthians 9:9)*

- The principle of _____ *(Proverbs 11:25)*

- The principle of misplaced trust *(Proverbs 11:28)*

- The principle of giving special gifts *(Deuteronomy 12:11-12)*

- The principle of _____ the greater blessing *(Acts 20:34-35)*

- The principle of placing our treasure *(Matthew 6:20-21)*

- The principle of generous giving *(II Corinthians 8:2)*

- The principle of _____ *(I Timothy 6:6-7)*

- The principle of leaving it all behind *(I Timothy 6:7)*

- The principle of foolish desires *(I Timothy 6:9-10)*

- The principle of not loving money *(I Timothy 6:10)*

- The principle of being humble *(I Timothy 6:17)*

- The principle of _____ in God *(I Timothy 6:17-18)*

- The principle of sharing *(I Timothy 6:18)*

- The principle of _____ *(I Timothy 6:20)*

- The principle of sacrifice *(Luke 21:4)*

- The principle of placing your needs last *(I Kings 17:9-16)*

- The principle of _____ others *(Genesis 12:2-3)*

- The principle of open floodgates *(Malachi 3:10)*

- The principle of excess blessing *(Malachi 3:10)*

- The principle of _____ protection *(Malachi 3:11-12)*

If we can make it happen on our own, there is no need for faith.

- The principle of transparent blessing *(Malachi 3:12)*

- The principle of first fruits *(Proverbs 3:9)*

- The principle of _____ barns *(Proverbs 3:10)*

- The principle of the first born *(Exodus 13:1-2)*

- The principle of God as Master *(Matthew 6:24)*

- The principle of _____ God *(Matthew 6:34)*

- The principle of resisting temptation *(Matthew 4:8-11)*

- The principle of a pure heart *(Matthew 5:8)*

- The principle of showing mercy *(Matthew 5:7)*

- The principle of _____ relationships *(Matthew 5:23-24)*

- The principle of correct giving *(Matthew 6:2)*

- The principle of understanding greed *(Luke 12:16-19)*

- The principle of _____ for family *(I Timothy 5:8)*

- The principle of lending to the Lord *(Proverbs 19:17)*

- The principle of righteous giving *(Proverbs 21:26)*

- The principle of lacking nothing *(Proverbs 28:27)*

- The principle of sharing coats *(Luke 3:11)*

- The principle of _____ in business *(Romans 12:11-12)*

You need to understand your calling and purpose in life and set out objectives that will allow you to live that fulfilled life.

- The principle of a cheerful giver *(II Corinthians 9:7)*

- The principle of sowing bountifully *(II Corinthians 9:6)*

- The principle of _____ all things *(I Timothy 6:17)*

- The principle of honoring the Lord *(Proverbs 3:9)*

- The principle of finding God's provision *(Matthew 17:27)*

- The principle of _____ from the love of money *(Hebrews 13:4-5)*

- The principle of knowing the Source *(I Chronicles 29:10-12)*

- The principle of the ultimate gift *(John 3:16, Romans 8:31-33)*

N O T E S

STUDENT RESPONSE

Improvement Action Plan

What I need to change: _____

What? I define my goal as this achievable result. What will be my final outcome?

My answer: _____

_____

Why? This is why I need to accomplish my goal.

My answer: _____

_____

Who? Who will be involved in making me successful?

My answer: _____

_____

Where? Where will I get started? In what area will I begin?

My answer: _____

_____

How? How will I accomplish what I want to achieve? How will I measure my progress?

My answer: _____

_____

When? When will I begin working on achieving this goal?

My answer: _____

_____

Lesson Five

PERSONA OF A STEWARD

"Having started the ball rolling so enthusiastically, you should carry this project through to completion just as gladly, giving whatever you can out of whatever you have. Let your enthusiastic idea at the start be equaled by your realistic action now."
II Corinthians 8:11 (TLB)

"The only gift is a portion of thyself."
Ralph Waldo Emerson

"I've seen you stalking the malls, walking the aisles, searching for that extra-special gift. Stashing away a few dollars a month to buy him some lizard-skin boots; staring at a thousand rings to find her the best diamond; staying up all night Christmas Eve, assembling the new bicycle. Why do you do it? So the eyes will pop, the jaw will drop. To hear those words of disbelief: 'You did this for me?' And that is why God did it. Next time a sunrise steals your breath or a meadow of flowers leaves you speechless, remain that way. Say nothing, and listen as heaven whispers, 'Do you like it? I did it just for you.'"
Max Lucado – The Great House of God (Word)

Lesson Five

PERSONA OF A STEWARD

1. **Introduction**

   a. Worldly priorities are to surround oneself with all the comforts the world has to offer, but this is not the _____ perspective.

   "Praise be to the God and Father of our Lord Jesus Christ, the Father of compassion and the God of all comfort, who comforts us in all our troubles, so that we can comfort those in any trouble with the comfort we ourselves have received from God. For just as the sufferings of Christ flow over into our lives, so also through Christ our comfort overflows. If we are distressed, it is for your comfort and salvation; if we are comforted, it is for your comfort, which produces in you patient endurance of the same sufferings we suffer. And our hope for you is firm, because we know that just as you share in our sufferings, so also you share in our comfort." (II Corinthians 1:3-7)

   b. The Bible teaches stewardship, that our _____ are not ours, but God's, and they have been given to us for a purpose.

   Mark 10:17-22

2. **Stewardship in Scripture**

   Genesis 1:28, Matthew 10:8

3. **Old Testament Stewardship**

   The steward of the Old Testament was given the task of _____ another's possessions or household. It was the number one servant, possessing a place of authority and accountability. The steward would later become the heir.

   Genesis 15:2, Genesis 24

4. **New Testament Stewardship**

Good stewards were rewarded with increased _____ and income, but a poor steward was disgraced or fired. A steward is held accountable.

Luke 16:1-13

5. **A Steward's Character**

Honest and Faithful

"Moreover it is required in stewards, that a man be found faithful." (1 Corinthians 4:2, KJV)

6. **Integrity Issues**

Integrity is "being _____, unimpaired, perfect condition, of sound moral principle, uprightness." (Webster's Dictionary)

"Better is the poor that walketh in his integrity, than he that is perverse in his lips, and is a fool." (Proverbs 19:1, KJV)

7. **The Whole Picture**

God is interested in the stewardship of not only our finances, but our _____ life.

8. **Planning Ahead**

"I tell you, use worldly wealth to gain friends for yourselves, so that when it is gone, you will be welcomed into eternal dwellings." (Luke 16:9)

The astute businessperson looks ahead and plans for the future. He or she manages money so as to provide benefits not only for the present, but for the future.

9. Acknowledging God

God owns the earth – _____ comes from Him.

1 Chronicles 29:13,14, Exodus 9:29, Isaiah 66:1,2, Acts 7:49,50, II Kings 19:15, Nehemiah 9:6, Jeremiah 27:5, Hebrews 1:10, Acts 17:24, Job 12:9-10, Psalm 89:11, Psalm 95:3-5, Daniel 4:17, John 19:11, Rev 4:11

10. God in Control

Romans 12:1

What does God already own that you are trying to keep absolute control over by refusing to acknowledge God's ownership?

11. Faithfulness

Be faithful to _____ the Lord when He asks something of you.

Deuteronomy 5:32

12. Oversight

When we are faithful, God allows us to be overseers of His property.

"For every beast of the forest is mine, and the cattle upon a thousand hills. I know all the fowls of the mountains: and the wild beasts of the field are mine." (Psalm 50:10,11, KJV)

13. Reflection

How we _____ our possessions must reflect God's interest.
Genesis 1:26, 2:15

14. Caring for God's Gifts

15. Reliability

16. Managing Our Possessions

"So if you have not been trustworthy in handling worldly wealth, who will trust you with true riches?" (Luke 16:11)

"His divine power has given us everything we need for life and godliness..." (2 Peter 1:3)

17. Unlimited Resources

18. Financial Control

19. Dominion over Creation

God gave us authority over creation, but we must _____ it through work.

"In the sweat of thy face shalt thou eat bread, till thou return unto the ground..." (Genesis 3:19, KJV)

"For even when we were with you, this we commanded you, that if any would not work, neither should he eat." (II Thessalonians 3:10, KJV)

20. Use of Personal Resources

Matthew 25:14-30

21. Working Hard

"Go to the ant, you sluggard; consider its ways and be wise! It has no commander, no overseer or ruler, yet it stores its provisions in summer and gathers its food at harvest. How long will you lie there, you sluggard? When will you get up from your sleep? A little sleep, a little slumber, a little folding of the hands to rest-- and poverty will come on you like a bandit and scarcity like an armed man." (Proverbs 6:6-11)

"Make it your ambition to lead a quiet life, to mind your own business and to work with your hands, just as we told you, so that your daily life may win the respect of outsiders and so that you will not be dependent on anybody." (I Thessalonians 4:11,12)

"Lazy hands make a man poor, but diligent hands bring wealth. He who gathers crops in summer is a wise son, but he who sleeps during harvest is a disgraceful son" (Proverbs 10:4,5)

"Do you see a man skilled in his work? He will serve before kings; he will not serve before obscure men." (Proverbs 22:29)

"Whatever your hand finds to do, do it with all your might..." (Ecclesiastes 9:10)

"A sluggard does not plow in season; so at harvest time he looks but finds nothing." (Proverbs 20:4)

22. The Virtue of Diligence

Give more than is required, go the second mile and the third and fourth.

23. Prosperous and Successful

When we apply biblical instruction, work hard and lead a _____ lifestyle, we will experience success in life.

24. Productive Stewardship

John 15:1-5

25. Developing God's Gifts

a. Idleness and _____ will be judged.

Ecclesiastes 10:18

b. We will give an account on judgement day.

Matthew 12:36

c. We can make good use of the _____ of time.

Ephesians 5:16

d. We are responsible for the development of God's gifts in us.

Matthew 25

NOTES

STUDENT RESPONSE

Improvement Action Plan

What I need to change: _____

What? I define my goal as this achievable result. What will be my final outcome?

My answer: _____

_____

Why? This is why I need to accomplish my goal.

My answer: _____

_____

Who? Who will be involved in making me successful?

My answer: _____

_____

Where? Where will I get started? In what area will I begin?

My answer: _____

_____

How? How will I accomplish what I want to achieve? How will I measure my progress?

My answer: _____

_____

When? When will I begin working on achieving this goal?

My answer: _____

_____

Lesson Six

DISCIPLINES OF A STEWARD

"Redeeming the time, because the days are evil."
EPHESIANS 5:16 (KJV)

"Go to the ant, you sluggard; consider its ways and be wise! It has no commander, no overseer or ruler, yet it stores its provisions in summer and gathers its food at harvest. How long will you lie there, you sluggard? When will you get up from your sleep? A little sleep, a little slumber, a little folding of the hands to rest—and poverty will come on you like a bandit and scarcity like an armed man."
PROVERBS 6:6-11

"Remember that time is money."
BENJAMIN FRANKLIN

"Knowledge is advantageous, skill is indispensable, experience is invaluable, communication is fundamental, enthusiasm is beneficial, attitude is essential—but personal discipline determines the level of your achievement."
RICH BROTT

Lesson Six

DISCIPLINES OF A STEWARD

1. **God's Gift of Time**

   a. As stewards, we must use time _____ and to our advantage in fulfilling our destiny.

   b. Time management takes self-control, perseverance and self-discipline, but this investment pays high dividends.

   c. We should consider budgeting and _____ our time, much as we do our finances.

   d. How we use our time counts.

2. **The Investment of Time**

   a. To _____ is to use something in such a way as to bring future benefits.

   b. Time carefully planned and invested will rarely be wasted.

3. **The Value of Time**

   Prioritize your time so that _____ matters will not be forgotten or left out.

4. **The Purpose of Time**

   It is not how much you do that counts, but how much has _____ and lasting benefit.

5. **The Bank of Time**

   Our time is an _____ that is replenished and then emptied daily.

6. **The Stewardship of Time**

   a. Plan your work.

   b. List your tasks.

   c. Develop a _____ work schedule.

   d. Do related jobs together.

   e. Learn to rest creatively.

7. **The Control of Time**

   Develop habits that put you in _____ of your time.

   "Before the mountains were born or you brought forth the earth and the world, from everlasting to everlasting you are God." (Psalms 90:2)

   "For a thousand years in your sight are like a day that has just gone by, or like a watch in the night." (Psalms 90:4)

   "The length of our days is seventy years—or eighty, if we have the strength; yet their span is but trouble and sorrow, for they quickly pass, and we fly away." (Psalms 90:10)

   "Teach us to number our days aright, that we may gain a heart of wisdom." (Psalms 90:12)

8. **God's Gift of Communication**

   "But to do good, and to communicate forget not: for with such sacrifices God is well pleased." (Hebrews 13:16, KJV)

   "And he said unto them, What manner of communications are these that ye have one to another, as ye walk, and are sad." (Luke 24:17, KJV)

   "But let your communication be, Yea, yea; Nay, nay: for whatsoever is more than these cometh of evil." (Matthew 5:37, KJV)

   "Let no corrupt communication proceed out of your mouth, but that which is good to the use of edifying, that it may minister grace unto the hearers." (Ephesians 4:29, KJV)

   "But now ye also put off all these; anger, wrath, malice, blasphemy, filthy communication out of your mouth." (Colossians 3:8, KJV)

"Be not deceived: evil communications corrupt good manners." (I Corinthians 15:33, KJV)

9. The Stewardship of Communication

Our ability to _____ with others is one of God's greatest gifts and often, one of our greatest challenges.

10. Defining Communication

(from Strong's Greek/Hebrew Dictionary and Vine's Expository Dictionary of Biblical Words)

a. Communication

    i.   Partnership, _____, social intercourse, communication, communion and fellowship

        Hebrews 13:16, Philemon 6

    ii.   A spoken word, communication, speech

        Luke 24:17, Matthew 5:37, Ephesians 4:29, Colossians 3:8

b. To Communicate

    i.   To have a share in, give a share to, _____ with, communicate, have fellowship with

        Romans 15:27, 1 Timothy 5:22, Hebrews 2:14, I Peter 4:13, II John 11, Romans 12:13, Galatians 6:6

    ii.   To share together with, communicate with, partake of, share with others to meet needs

        Philippians 4:14, Ephesians 5:11, Revelation 18:4

c. Communicative: Apt/ _____ to Communicate

    1 Timothy 6:18

11. The Cycle of Communication

Communication is the sending and receiving of information among people.

a. What You _____ to Say

   b. What You Really Say

   c. What the Other Person Hears

   d. What the Other Person _____ (S)He Heard

   e. What the Other Person Says about What You Said

   f. What You Think the Other Person _____ about What You Said

12. Communication Difficulties

   a. Words mean different things to different people.

   b. Learn to be _____ and reflective in communication.

13. Benefits of Communication

   a. Careful listening is enormously beneficial.

   b. Identify the sender's _____ idea by keeping your own ideas in the background.

   c. Concentrate on what the sender is saying.

14. Communication and Emotion

   a. Delay _____ of the message until after it is completed.

   b. Do not reject what you hear as too familiar, unfamiliar or trivial.

   c. Pay _____ not only to the words, but also what is being communicated in other ways.

   d. Do not formulate arguments against the sender's ideas before you fully understand them.

15. Maximizing Communication

   a. Ignore _____ surroundings.

   b. Do not refuse to listen to difficult or complicated information.

16. Communication Connections

   a. Look for points of agreement and _____ points of interest.

   b. Words like "but" and "you" can inhibit good conversation.

17. Styles of Communication

    a. Your style of communication should have a positive effect on others.

    b. Try to make most of your communication _____ for others.

    c. Learn to put others at ease.

18. Partners in Communication

Treat communication like a _____ between two or more individuals.

19. Positive Communication

    a. Choose positive words to make positive _____ as easy as possible.

    b. Try not to use generalizations.

20. Communication Styles

    a. Be aware of _____ communication behaviors or styles.

    b. Develop positive communication behaviors or styles.

21. Conclusion

Our stewardship of time and _____ will have a direct effect on our finances.

NOTES

S T U D E N T   R E S P O N S E

Improvement Action Plan

What I need to change: _____

What? I define my goal as this achievable result. What will be my final outcome?

My answer: _____

_____

Why? This is why I need to accomplish my goal.

My answer: _____

_____

Who? Who will be involved in making me successful?

My answer: _____

_____

Where? Where will I get started? In what area will I begin?

My answer: _____

_____

How? How will I accomplish what I want to achieve? How will I measure my progress?

My answer: _____

_____

When? When will I begin working on achieving this goal?

My answer: _____

_____

Lesson Seven

HOW TO MAKE WISE FAMILY DECISIONS

"If only they were wise and would understand this and discern what their end will be!"
DEUTERONOMY 32:29

"I asked God for strength, that I might achieve.
I was made weak, that I might learn humbly to obey...
I asked for health, that I might do greater things.
I was given infirmity, that I might do better things..
I asked for riches, that I might be happy.
I was given poverty, that I might be wise...
I asked for power, that I might have the praise of men.
I was given weakness, that I might feel the need of God...
I asked for all things that I might enjoy life.
I was given life, that I might enjoy all things...
I got nothing I asked for – but everything I had hoped for.
Almost despite myself, my unspoken prayers were answered.
I am among men, most richly blessed!"
ROY CAMPANELLA, BASEBALL PLAYER

Lesson Seven

HOW TO MAKE WISE FAMILY DECISIONS

1. Introduction

a. Before thinking about long-term investment strategies, you must _____ the decision-making process.

b. Decision-making is necessary to function effectively.

Making decisions about financial affairs demands conscious attention to one's goals as well as to one's money.

---

c. Not all actions result from decisions, some result from habit.

d. Money _____ can also result from habit or impulse.

2. How a Decision Occurs

A decision occurs when a _____ is consciously made and acted upon after weighing the facts and examining the alternatives and their outcomes. A decision can alter one's life as its effects continue on into the future.

3. Characteristics of Decisions

a. Decisions are interrelated.

Once a decision is made, it sets in motion a chain reaction of further decisions.

b. Making a _____ involves risk.

The outcome of a decision cannot always be predicted though we base it on all the facts available and upon the best advice.

A decision has a history; that is, it is related to a past and to a future.

c. Decisions cause change.

A change in _____ may precede the decision.

d. Decisions require commitment.

   i. Without a serious commitment to one's goal, the drastic attitude and behavior changes – which are sometimes necessary – will hinder your _____ of that goal.

   ii. Decisions make demands that require self-discipline.

e. Decisions involve cost.

The cost of a financial decision can be difficult to accept and live with, because when money is used to reach your goals, there is less to use for other things.

4. Three-Step Process

a. Seek _____ solutions.

b. Weigh the alternatives.

Information must be gathered about costs; alternatives cannot be accurately judged unless enough is known about them.

c. Make a choice.

   i. A choice is made based on personal goals and available resources.

   ii. The decision is put into action by _____ the necessary resources and activities.

iii.   Once the _____ has been made, no second-guessing!

5. Effectiveness of a Decision

The effectiveness of a decision is measured by whether or not it helps accomplish whatever one sets out to do.

---

a. If a desired _____ is being hindered, a decision may need to be re-evaluated.

b. Decisions involving finance require specific knowledge and information.

c. Decisions with long-term effects require _____ thought.

6. Five Steps to Family Decisions

a. Recall past experience.

Avoid making _____ you've made in the past.

b. Keep financial records.

When considering a new financial commitment, it is necessary to know how it may affect commitments that have already been made.

c. Borrow _____ from people you know.

When doing something for the first time, i.e. buying a house, investing for the future, ask someone who's already done it for advice.

d. Look up specific information.

Use the library and the Internet; background information and understanding are essential in choosing a course of action.

e. Consult professionals and experts. _____ your decisions regularly and plan for difficulties you may face in the future.

NOTES

STUDENT RESPONSE

Improvement Action Plan

What I need to change: _____

What? I define my goal as this achievable result. What will be my final outcome?

My answer: _____

_____

Why? This is why I need to accomplish my goal.

My answer: _____

_____

Who? Who will be involved in making me successful?

My answer: _____

_____

Where? Where will I get started? In what area will I begin?

My answer: _____

_____

How? How will I accomplish what I want to achieve? How will I measure my progress?

My answer: _____

_____

When? When will I begin working on achieving this goal?

My answer: _____

_____

Lesson Eight

FACING FINANCIAL CHALLENGES

"Give us counsel, render a decision... "
ISAIAH 16:3

"Alas, how many, even among those who are called believers, have plenty of all the necessities of life, and yet complain of poverty!"
JOHN WESLEY

"I do not pray for success. I ask for faithfulness."
MOTHER TERESA

Lesson Eight

FACING FINANCIAL CHALLENGES

1. **Inevitable Challenges**

   Families are faced with many financial challenges and decision-making opportunities. Various resources can be used to solve these problems and to achieve individual family goals. Tackle one problem at a time. You will find _____ in being in control of your financial life. Let's look at some steps toward solving financial challenges.

2. **Seeking Improvement**

   The process starts with _____ the difference between what is and what ought to be and then wanting to do something about it.

3. **Clarifying Goals**

   Prioritize your family's financial goals and rate them as to importance.

4. **Defining the Problem**

   State and carefully _____ the obstacle(s) to each goal.

5. **Determining Resources**

   Examine what human and material resources are available; these all have potential to generate additional income to meet a specific family goal.

6. **Outlining Alternatives**

   a. Outline all alternatives and _____ each in terms of its outcome.

   b. Special information or assistance from experts should be obtained when a solution involves large amounts of money.

STUDENT RESPONSE

Improvement Action Plan

What I need to change: _____

What? I define my goal as this achievable result. What will be my final outcome?

My answer: _____

_____

Why? This is why I need to accomplish my goal.

My answer: _____

_____

Who? Who will be involved in making me successful?

My answer: _____

_____

Where? Where will I get started? In what area will I begin?

My answer: _____

_____

How? How will I accomplish what I want to achieve? How will I measure my progress?

My answer: _____

_____

When? When will I begin working on achieving this goal?

My answer: _____

_____

Lesson Nine

DEFINING YOUR FINANCIAL FUTURE

"Brothers, I do not consider myself yet to have taken hold of it. But one thing I do: Forgetting what is behind and straining toward what is ahead, I press on toward the goal..."
PHILIPPIANS 3:13, 14

"If you don't know where you're going, you'll end up somewhere else."
YOGI BERRA

"Destiny is not a matter of chance, it is a matter of choice; it is not a thing to be waited for, it is a thing to be achieved."
WILLIAM JENNINGS BRYAN

"Success is the progressive realization of a worthy goal."
EARL NIGHTINGALE

Lesson Nine

DEFINING YOUR FINANCIAL FUTURE

1. **Defining Purpose**

   Write a statement of purpose – a general mission or vision statement that describes the overall intent that governs your goals, _____, strategies and activities.

2. **Defining Objectives**

   Determine the results you desire to achieve.

3. **Defining Goals**

   Determine your goals based upon your personal values.

4. **Analyzing My Goals**

   Determine the suitability of your goals based on your life circumstances.

5. **Purpose Precedes Goals**

   To discover purpose in life, define objectives and achieve personal and professional goals, you must be _____ in your personal commitment to the planning task at hand.

Start now by defining your purpose, your life philosophy, your objectives and then your goals.

---

6. **Dangerous Complacency**

   Success requires that we _____ challenge ourselves.

7. **Achievable Goals**

    a. Determine direction of activity (purpose).

    b. Focus on the _____ (objectives).

    c. Measure at determined checkpoints (planning).

    d. Establish a _____ for results (completion).

8. **Necessary Challenges**

Set a course of achievement and reward for your life.

9. **Risking Another Bump**

When we – despite the risk of experiencing some failure – strive to reach our full _____, we will reach it and inspire others to do the same.

10. **Why Goals Are Not Set**

    a. Goals are never set by some because of the fear of failure.

    b. Many do not set goals because of lack of _____ to stay with the task until it becomes a reality.

    c. Others are professional procrastinators.

11. **Take the Procrastinator Test.**

Answer each question with one of the responses on the following continuum: never (1 point); some times (2); half the time (3); most of the time (4); always (5). How often do I...?

    a. Put off doing something I have to get done?

    b. Wait to move until someone forces or strongly encourages me to do something?

    c. Look for reasons (or excuses) not to do something I should do?

    d. Fail to complete projects I've started?

e. Allow myself pleasant indulgences (over-sleeping, over-eating, skipping responsibilities, etc.)?

f. Find that I've run out of time to complete a project properly because I didn't start soon enough?

g. Allow obstacles and difficulties to prevent me from completing a project?

Add up your score and see how you rate!

7-9 If you're so conscientious, why aren't you working?

10-18 You're starting to sound truthful.

19-25 With a little practice, you might never get anything done.

26-34 How did you get around to finishing this test?

35 You're hopeless!

12. The Caterpillar Complex

Be careful not to define your goals on the aimless direction of others.

13. A Worthwhile Goal

Goal setting should bring out the best in a person, allowing him to stretch.

14. Effective Goals that Last

Goals that endure are: visualized, achievable, written, measurable, manageable, reviewed, reviewed, deadline-oriented, and rewarded.

15. Achieving Improvement

Clarity of purpose and direction is instrumental to improvement.

Don't drift through life... be purposeful!

16. Having Clear Goals

    a. Focuses the Mind

    b. Channels Energy

    c. Gives _____ to Your Life

    d. Requires Commitment to Accomplish Specific Things

    e. Provides Motivation

    f. Makes Reaching Goals _____ Forming

    g. Generates New Goal Setting When Results Are Achieved

17. Focusing on Your Financial Goals

    a. Short-Term Financial Goals

    b. Intermediate _____ Goals

    c. Long-Range Financial Goals

    d. The Hierarchy of Goals

18. Setting Financial Goals

    a. It gives you control.

    b. It points you in the _____ direction.

    c. It helps you know yourself.

    d. It keeps you on track.

    e. It helps you to _____ financial assets.

    f. It helps you prepare for retirement.

    g. It helps with educational expenses.

    h. It _____ you for the unexpected.

    i. It improves family communication.

19. Steps to Goal Setting

    a. Write down your financial goals.

    b. Give yourself a deadline.

    c. Set your _____ high.

    d. Get realistic, obtainable goals.

e. Be _____ and specific.

f. Be flexible.

g. Begin with the first step.

20. Overview of Goals

21. The Planning Process

a. Though it may seem intimidating or overwhelming, once you start _____ ahead and building a solid financial strategy for success, it becomes easier.

b. Planning is knowing where you are today, outlining the steps it will take to reach your financial goals, _____ a sound plan and continuing to follow the pattern you outlined until your goals are met.

The planning process is no better than the goal, the goal is no better than the objective, and the objective is no better than the purpose or reason for existing.

---

22. Why Plan?

a. To Achieve Your Financial Goals

b. To Put Your _____ to Work

c. To Be Prepared

d. To Cope with Change

e. To Be in Control

f. To Decide What You Want to Do with Your Money

g. To Decide How Your Money Should _____ for You

23. Take Time to Plan

Good planning is essential to meeting financial goals.

24. Planning Checklist

    a.   Set specific _____ of progress.

    b.   Outline procedures.

    c.   Assign activities.

25. Quality Planning

    a.   Importance

    b.   Constructing the Plan

    c.   Following the Plan

    d.   Evaluating the Plan

    e.   Revising and _____ the Plan

NOTES

S T U D E N T   R E S P O N S E

Improvement Action Plan

What I need to change: _____

What? I define my goal as this achievable result. What will be my final outcome?

My answer: _____

_____

Why? This is why I need to accomplish my goal.

My answer: _____

_____

Who? Who will be involved in making me successful?

My answer: _____

_____

Where? Where will I get started? In what area will I begin?

My answer: _____

_____

How? How will I accomplish what I want to achieve? How will I measure my progress?

My answer: _____

_____

When? When will I begin working on achieving this goal?

My answer: _____

_____

Lesson Ten

MANAGING YOUR CASH FLOW

"When that year was over, they came to him the following year and said, 'We cannot hide from our lord the fact that since our money is gone and our livestock belongs to you, there is nothing left for our lord except our bodies and our land.'"
GENESIS 47:18

"Ultimately, it's not what you earn that gives you financial security, but what you save."

*"It is not what you'd do with a million
If riches should e'er be your lot.
But what you are doing at present
With the dollar and a quarter you've got."*
R.G. LeTourneau

Lesson Ten

MANAGING YOUR CASH FLOW

1. Managing Cash Flow by Finding Missing Money

   a. A system to _____ for spending and cash flow is necessary.

   b. Check stubs, receipts and charge account statements paint the big picture, but pocket money must also be accounted for.

   c. It's easy to stumble, make wrong choices and let go of personal _____, but you can get back on track.

2. Managing Cash Flow by Recording Spending

   a. Getting an Easy Start

      Record daily _____ in a pocket-sized journal.

   b. Setting up Expense Categories

      i.   Determine narrow expense categories for the most detailed _____ of monthly spending.

      ii.   Enter these into a simple ledger pad ruled with one wide column and at least six columns on the right for entering figures.

      iii. Recognize which expenses are _____ and which are variable.

      iv. Record savings, preferably 10% or more of your income, as a fixed expense that you "pay yourself" monthly.

      v.   Record fixed expenses directly in the ledger and variable expenses once a month (as taken from the _____ journal).

      vi. Label each page of the journal with the categories.

   c. Keeping Good Spending Records

      Record each day's expenses in the right category every evening.

   d. Totaling the Spending

    i.   Total the specific _____ and record your journal each month and each total in the ledger.

Tune in to what you are spending!

---

    ii.   When the daily journal is properly kept, monthly totaling should take only a half-hour.

    iii.   If your expenses exceeded your income, consider what _____ spending you could cut down on the next month.

e. Staying with the Process

Repeat the process for three to six months.

f. Record-Keeping Basics

    i.   Income

    ii.   Salary

    iii.   Accuracy

    iv.   Continuity

g. Tracking the Little Stuff

    i.   Keeping track of small change, turns casual _____ into a conscious, ordered process by linking the act of spending money with the act of recording the expense.

    ii.   After three to six months of recording, your ledger page becomes a _____ model of your finances over time.

    iii.   Consider using Excel spreadsheets or investing in a money management program for your computer.

iv.   As you develop this system, you will find yourself setting goals and establishing priorities, the necessary _____ for a realistic personal financial plan.

3. Managing Cash Flow by Right Spending

a. Tithe and Savings First

b. Living Expenses Next

c. Debt Reduction

d. Wants Last

4. Managing Cash Flow by Watching the Cash

a. Accounting and budgeting will assist you in managing your financial picture.

NOTES

STUDENT RESPONSE

Improvement Action Plan

What I need to change: _____

What? I define my goal as this achievable result. What will be my final outcome?

My answer: _____

_____

Why? This is why I need to accomplish my goal.

My answer: _____

_____

Who? Who will be involved in making me successful?

My answer: _____

_____

Where? Where will I get started? In what area will I begin?

My answer: _____

_____

How? How will I accomplish what I want to achieve? How will I measure my progress?

My answer: _____

_____

When? When will I begin working on achieving this goal?

My answer: _____

_____

Lesson Eleven

FINANCIAL BENEFITS OF BUDGETING

"Suppose one of you wants to build a tower. Will he not first sit down and estimate the cost to see if he has enough money to complete it?"
LUKE 14:28

"Persistence is stubbornness with a purpose."
RICHARD DEVOS, CO-FOUNDER, AMWAY

Lesson Eleven

Financial Benefits of Budgeting

1. **Introduction**

   a. Families who have everything under control and who are financially _____ still need a budget.

   b. When we spend more than we earn, the lack of money can contribute to much unhappiness.

   c. Properly managed money can _____ family relationships.

   d. Preparation of a meaningful budget depends on keeping accurate records.

Budgets aren't records of expenses, they are forecasts of expenses.

---

2. **Principles**

   • Budgeting is a _____ for managing money.

   • Budgeting stops unnecessary spending.

   • Budgeting helps you break bad habits.

   • Budgeting _____ the door to financial security.

   • Budgeting gives your family a spending plan.

   • Budgeting will help you get in shape financially.

   • Budgeting helps you _____ the money you earn.

   • Budgeting will help you become debt-free.

   • Budgeting will free you, not confine you.

   "The mind of man plans his way, but the Lord directs his steps."
   (Proverbs 16:9)

119

- Budgeting is scriptural.

  "Know well the condition of your flocks, and pay attention to your herds." (Proverbs 27:23)

- Budgeting is a _____ effort.

- Budgeting will make you disciplined.

- A budget for family spending gives order to family money.

- Budgeting gives you financial _____ and order.

- A budget for family spending provides a blueprint for reaching goals.

- A budget systematizes one's money affairs and aids in accomplishing goals.

- A budget begins with a statement of family income.

- A budget informs you of the fixed _____ to which the family is committed.

- A budget provides for the necessary variable expenses.

- A budget will help you with the big-ticket purchases.

- Budgeting helps you prepare in advance.

- Budgeting helps you attain special _____.

- Budgeting gives you another chance.

- Budgeting is tailor-made for your family.

- Budgeting makes your money do what you want it to.

  i)   All goals must be based _____ on your projected budget.

  ii)   Provide for the basics first, then the comforts, and finally the luxuries.

  iii) Set up a plan for paying off debts already accumulated.

  iv)   Plan for savings, no matter how small. Increase your savings allocation as your old debts are reduced.

  v)   Control your spending according to your budget.

  vi)   Never give in to _____ to depart from the budget.

  vii) If you stumble, don't give up; regroup and get on task again.

- Budgeting is an effective management tool.

- Budgeting gives you a financial blueprint.

- Budgeting allows you to know what is going on.

- Budgeting _____ you financial control.

- Budgeting provides organization.

- Budgeting encourages communication.

- A budget allows you to take _____ of opportunities.

- Budgeting offers you extra time.

- Budgeting brings you extra money.

NOTES

STUDENT RESPONSE

Improvement Action Plan

What I need to change: _____

What? I define my goal as this achievable result. What will be my final outcome?

My answer: _____

_____

Why? This is why I need to accomplish my goal.

My answer: _____

_____

Who? Who will be involved in making me successful?

My answer: _____

_____

Where? Where will I get started? In what area will I begin?

My answer: _____

_____

How? How will I accomplish what I want to achieve? How will I measure my progress?

My answer: _____

_____

When? When will I begin working on achieving this goal?

My answer: _____

_____

Lesson Twelve

DESIGNING THAT PERFECT BUDGET

"Make it your ambition to lead a quiet life, to mind your own business and to work with your hands, just as we told you, so that your daily life may win the respect of outsiders and so that you will not be dependent on anybody."
I THESSALONIANS 4:11,12

"Never spend your money before you have it."
THOMAS JEFFERSON (1743 – 1826)

Lesson Twelve

DESIGNING THAT PERFECT BUDGET

1. **First Steps to Wealth**

   a. Take control of your income and outgo.

   b. Be in _____ of your financial future.

2. **How Do I Get Started?**

   a. First, categorize and list all regular expenses.

   b. Next, fill in the blanks on the spreadsheet.

   c. Try to better _____ your expenses, but don't forget to ask God for guidance.

   Jeremiah 17:7, 8; James 4:10

3. **Making Your Budget Work**

   Consider setting up a budget _____ with your expense categories in the left column and fifteen additional columns.

   Column 1 – amount budgeted per month per category

   Columns 2-13 – January through December actual costs

   Column 14 – total annual costs

   Column 15 – average monthly costs

A budget is a powerful method of gaining control, planning, communicating, and fulfilling your dreams.

---

4. **Some Budgeting Tips**

    a. Be patient.

    b. Invest or _____ any windfall income.

    c. If you have a quarterly, semiannual or annual payment, save that amount each month so it doesn't throw off your budget.

    d. Don't forget to pay yourself. Save something each month that can go toward an investment.

    e. Don't try to track every penny – it will drive you and everyone else nuts.

    f. Make _____ buying difficult – leave your checkbook and credit cards at home.

    g. Set aside some fun money for each family member.

    h. Budget for fun (vacation, toy).

    i. Don't over-categorize (too many expense categories).

    j. Don't use her paycheck for certain things and his for others.

    k. Use an _____ checking account.

    l. Record savings as an expense item.

    m. Create an "expense" item to pay off credit-card balances.

    n. Pay off cards with the highest interest rate first.

    o. Don't use credit cards again until the _____ is paid off.

    p. Once a loan is paid off, keep paying the amount to yourself (make a vacation fund or car fund).

    q. Set aside money monthly for bills due quarterly, semi-annually, or yearly.

    r. Reconcile your _____ at least once a month when reconciling your checking statement.

    s. Make sure to mark your last reconcile point in your budget.

    t. Just identifying your expenses is extremely valuable.

5. How to Organize Your Monthly, Quarterly and Annual Bills

    a. Pay your bills _____ to avoid late fees.

    b. Follow basic steps to keep you from procrastination.

    c. Always put your bills in a specific place when they arrive.

    d. Set aside _____ times a month, two weeks apart, to pay bills.

    e. Ask the companies that bill you to revise your payment due dates to correspond with one of these two times.

    f. Mark bill-paying dates on your calendar and pay on schedule.

    g. Pay with checks or money orders and _____ the check number, date, and amount you paid on the payment receipt.

    h. File payment receipts and keep them for up to seven years.

    i. Place payment envelopes next to your car or house keys so you _____ to mail them immediately.

    j. Don't forget to take them all the way to the mailbox!

    k. Check due dates for bills as soon as they arrive in the mail, as this can sometimes change.

6. Why Budgets Fail

    a. Unrealistic Goals

    b. Quitting Too Soon

    c. Misunderstanding What a _____ Really Is

    d. Family Or Spousal Strife

    e. Going to Extremes

    f. The "More-Money-In, More-Money-Out" Syndrome

    g. Thinking That a Little _____ Won't Hurt

    h. Using Automatic Checking Account Overdrafts

    i. Misuse of Automatic Teller Machines (ATM)

    j. Refusing to Balance Your Checkbook

    k. The Common Feeling of Simple Discouragement

    l. Wrong _____: "I Don't Have Enough Money to Budget!"

    m. Not Teaching Your Children

"Instruct them to do good, to be rich in good works, to be generous and ready to share, storing up for themselves the treasure of a good foundation for the future, so that they may take hold of that which is life indeed." (I Timothy 6:18-19)

N O T E S

STUDENT RESPONSE

Improvement Action Plan

What I need to change: _____

What? I define my goal as this achievable result. What will be my final outcome?

My answer: _____

_____

Why? This is why I need to accomplish my goal.

My answer: _____

_____

Who? Who will be involved in making me successful?

My answer: _____

_____

Where? Where will I get started? In what area will I begin?

My answer: _____

_____

How? How will I accomplish what I want to achieve? How will I measure my progress?

My answer: _____

_____

When? When will I begin working on achieving this goal?

My answer: _____

_____

Lesson Thirteen

DEVELOPING THE SAVINGS HABIT

"The plans of the diligent lead to profit as surely as haste leads to poverty."
PROVERBS 21:5

"Diamonds are nothing more than chunks of coal that stuck to their job."
MALCOLM FORBES, PUBLISHER, FORBES MAGAZINE

Lesson Thirteen

DEVELOPING THE SAVINGS HABIT

1. Strategy

    a. First, put your money into a rainy-day fund.

    b. Save for _____ expenses.

    c. Save for retirement.

    d. Set up automatic payroll deduction.

    e. Set up automatic bank transfers.

    f. Invest _____ in salary.

    g. Invest lump sum payments like tax refunds and bonuses.

2. You Can Begin Saving Now

    a. Set savings goals.

    b. Pay yourself first.

    c. Throw _____ blocks in the path of spending.

    d. Save all extra money.

3. You Can Make Your Savings Grow Faster

    a. Money Market Funds

    b. Stock _____ Funds

    c. US Treasuries

4. How you Can Save

    a. Develop new habits.

    c. Don't buy on impulse.

    d. Get rid of _____ card debt.

    e. Use installment credit sparingly.

    f. Take good care of your assets.

    g. Update your homeowner's insurance policy.

h. Update your life insurance policy.

i. Start a _____ fund.

j. Get the best health insurance possible.

k. Pay off your mortgage faster.

l. Use non-money resources.

m. Develop good _____ habits.

n. Choose quality over price.

o. Pause before purchasing and ask. . .

    i. Can I really _____ it?

    ii. Do I really need it?

    iii. Is it worth what I'm paying?

o. Save by _____ things yourself.

    i. Wash your car yourself.

    ii. Review insurance policies to avoid overlapping coverage.

    iii. Buy a used car.

    iv. Eat out for _____ instead of dinner.

    v. Trade down in suits, travel arrangements, rental car size.

    vi. Look for a package when planning a trip.

    vii. Don't dispose of clothing you are tired of. Put it away for a season or two and you will _____ it again later.

    viii. Turn down the thermostat during winter and wear a sweater.

    ix. Buy holiday items after Christmas at half price and save them.

    x. Turn off the lights when you leave a room.

    xi. Jog or use public _____ areas instead of paying for a gym.

    xii. Save unused gifts with the giver's name and give to someone else a year later.

    xiii. Use _____ and low-cost offers/coupons.

    xiv. Borrow books at the library instead of buying them.

    xv. Use plastic/paper bags from the store as garbage bags.

    xvi. Return bottles and cans to the store and receive your deposit.

xvii.   Reuse paper clips.

xviii. Cut your own hair and that of family members.

xix.   Trade hand-me-downs with friends and relatives

p. Exercise _____ discipline.

q. Understand inflation.

Item Purchased Today	Cost in 20 Years (4.5% average annual inflation rate)	Cost in 20 Years (3.5% average annual inflation rate)
Coffee & Scone - $7	$16.88	$13.93
Steak for 1 - $20	$48.23	$39.80
A Weekend Away - $500	$1,205.86	$994.89

r. The Power of _____ Interest

s. Begin while you're young.

t. Learn how to invest.

NOTES

STUDENT RESPONSE

Improvement Action Plan

What I need to change: _____

What? I define my goal as this achievable result. What will be my final outcome?

My answer: _____

_____

Why? This is why I need to accomplish my goal.

My answer: _____

_____

Who? Who will be involved in making me successful?

My answer: _____

_____

Where? Where will I get started? In what area will I begin?

My answer: _____

_____

How? How will I accomplish what I want to achieve? How will I measure my progress?

My answer: _____

_____

When? When will I begin working on achieving this goal?

My answer: _____

_____

Lesson Fourteen

BORROWING AND CREDIT ISSUES

"Just as the rich rule the poor, so the borrower is servant to the lender."
PROVERBS 22:7 (TLB)

Lesson Fourteen

BORROWING AND CREDIT ISSUES

1. Do You Borrow Too Quickly?

God wants to _____ Himself as our Provider.

"Not that I am looking for a gift, but I am looking for what may be credited to your account. I have received full payment and even more; I am amply supplied, now that I have received from Epaphroditus the gifts you sent. They are a fragrant offering, an acceptable sacrifice, pleasing to God. And my God will meet all your needs according to his glorious riches in Christ Jesus." (Philippians 4:17-19)

"Let the wicked forsake his way and the evil man his thoughts. Let him turn to the LORD, and He will have mercy on him, and to our God, for He will freely pardon. 'For My thoughts are not your thoughts, neither are your ways My ways,' declares the LORD. 'As the heavens are higher than the earth, so are My ways higher than your ways and My thoughts than your thoughts.'" (Isaiah 55:7-9)

a. Getting into _____ is simple.

In essence, you slide into debt and have to climb out. Easy in, difficult to get out of.

---

b. The Lifestyle of Debt

c. Borrowing Money with the _____ Intentions

"Obey the laws, then, for two reasons: first, to keep from being punished, and second, just because you know you should. Pay your

taxes too, for these same two reasons. For government workers need to be paid so that they can keep on doing God's work, serving you. Pay everyone whatever he ought to have: pay your taxes and import duties gladly, obey those over you, and give honor and respect to all those to whom it is due. Pay all your debts except the debt of love for others— never finish paying that! For if you love them, you will be obeying all of God's laws, fulfilling all his requirement." (Romans 13:5-8, TLB)

"The wicked borrow and do not repay, but the righteous give generously." (Psalms 37:21)

d. Living a _____ Lifestyle

"Now the overseer must be above reproach... temperate, self-controlled, respectable..." (I Timothy 3:2)

"Thus says the LORD, your Redeemer, the Holy One of Israel: 'I am the LORD your God, who teaches you to profit, who leads you by the way you should go." (Isaiah 48:17, NKJ)

e. The _____ of Easy Credit

"Now listen, you who say, 'Today or tomorrow we will go to this or that city, spend a year there, carry on business and make money.' Why, you do not even know what will happen tomorrow. What is your life? You are a mist that appears for a little while and then vanishes. Instead, you ought to say, 'If it is the Lord's will, we will live and do this or that.'" (James 4:13-15)

Cultivate the mindset that you will only borrow for absolute necessities.

f. The _____ of Debt

"The rich rule over the poor, and the borrower is servant to the lender." (Proverbs 22:7)

g. Is credit debt dangerous?

h. Secrets of _____ Less

i. Pledge Yourself to Delayed Gratification

j. Credit Card Debt

k. Credit Card Interest

l. Warning Signs _____ Financial Disaster

"The alien who lives among you will rise above you higher and higher, but you will sink lower and lower. He will lend to you, but you will not lend to him. He will be the head, but you will be the tail." (Deuteronomy 28:43-45)

m. How can I get help?

"So I say to you: Ask and it will be given to you; seek and you will find; knock and the door will be opened to you. For everyone who asks receives; he who seeks finds; and to him who knocks, the door will be opened." (Luke 11:9-10)

n. The Importance of Being Credit-Worthy

o. Managing Your _____ Intelligently

p. How much debt is too much?

q. Breaking Free from the Spending Habit

r. Credit cards are not an _____ of your paycheck.

s. Paying as You Go

t. How to Avoid Excessive Debt

u. Owing More than Your Assets

v. Talk with Your Creditors

w. A _____ Credit Record

2. How Credit Reports Work

a. Identifying Information

b. Credit Information

    c. Public Record Information

    d. Inquiries

    e. How is credit _____ used?

    f. Only data is analyzed.

3. How To Improve Your Credit Score

    a. Close _____ you're not using.

    b. Don't hit all your credit limits.

    c. Manage inquiries into your record.

    d. Automate to be on time.

    e. Don't allow _____ payments.

    f. Check your credit report.

    g. Beware of mistakes.

    h. Beware of _____ credit cleaning companies.

4. Credit Scoring

    a. Payment History (35%)

    b. Outstanding Debt (30%)

    c. Length of Your Credit History (15%)

    d. Types of Credit in Use (10%)

    e. Recent Inquiries (10%)

    f. The _____ of Scores

5. How To Get Higher Credit Scores

    a. Pay your bills on time.

    b. Keep credit card _____ low.

    c. Keep no more than one or two credit cards.

    d. Make sure your credit records are accurate.

6. Why Do I Have Credit Problems?

Creditors evaluate borrowers upon character, capacity, and collateral.

7. **What Is Less than Perfect Credit?**

    a. Revolving or Installment Credit (e.g. Credit Card, Car Loan)

       More than two 30-days (or one 60-days) past-due payments

    b. Housing Debt - Any past-due payments

8. **Rebuilding Credit FAQ's**

    a. How to _____ Your Credit Rating

    b. Cleaning up Your Credit Report

    c. Obtaining a Copy of Your Credit Report

       You will need to provide the following information to the three major

       credit bureaus – Equifax, Trans Union and Experian:

       i.   Your full name (include Jr., Sr., III, etc.)

       ii. Your birth date

       iii. Your social security number

       iv. Your spouse's name

       v.   Your telephone number

       vi. Your five-year address history

    d. What should I do if I find _____ in my credit report?

    e. What can I do to rebuild my credit?

9. **Debt Consolidation**

    a. Don't Consolidate If…

       i.   Your habits will not change.

       ii. The interest rate to _____ will be high.

    b. Seriously Consider Consolidating to…

       i.   Stop creditor harassment.

       ii. Lower monthly payments.

       iii. Reduce interest and late fee charges.

NOTES

STUDENT RESPONSE

Improvement Action Plan

What I need to change: _____

What? I define my goal as this achievable result. What will be my final outcome?

My answer: _____

_____

Why? This is why I need to accomplish my goal.

My answer: _____

_____

Who? Who will be involved in making me successful?

My answer: _____

_____

Where? Where will I get started? In what area will I begin?

My answer: _____

_____

How? How will I accomplish what I want to achieve? How will I measure my progress?

My answer: _____

_____

When? When will I begin working on achieving this goal?

My answer: _____

_____

Lesson Fifteen

GETTING OUT
OF DEBT

"No discipline seems pleasant at the time, but painful. Later on, however, it produces a harvest of... peace for those who have been trained by it."
HEBREWS 12:11

"Creditors have better memories than debtors."
BENJAMIN FRANKLIN (1706 - 1790), POOR RICHARD'S ALMANAC (1758)

Lesson Fifteen

GETTING OUT OF DEBT

Perform a simple financial check-up to ensure that you are not headed for serious trouble.

1. **Actions – Not Just Good Intentions**

   By looking at your income and _____ for the past month, you can roughly determine your financial health.

2. **Danger Signals of Too Much Debt**

   Debt problems can be spotted before they become serious, so take a look!

3. **Do You Have a Credit Problem?**

   Most people need to borrow at some point and a good credit rating is _____ for fulfilling most financial goals in life.

Your credit rating is very important and must be protected at all costs.

---

4. **Forming Good Habits vs. Bad Habits**

   Let your _____ work for you, not against you.

5. **Small Efforts Equal Huge Rewards**

   Small changes we make can have significant effects when maintained over a long period of time.

6. **A Lesson Learned**

   Accomplishing great things does not require acts of _____,

   but only small, consistent, and determined steps toward a goal.

7. **A Simple Guide to Climbing Out of Debt**

8. **Determine Not to Overspend**

   This chart shows the difference made by a _____

   change like making your own lunch one extra day a week.

Number of Days Eating Out for Lunch	Number of Days Making Your Lunch	Total Lunch Expense	Annual Lunch Expense
5 days per week	0 days per week	$35.	$1,750
4 days per week	1 day per week	$29	$1,450
3 days per week	2 days per week	$23	$1,150
2 days per week	3 days per week	$17	$850
1 day per week	4 days per week	$11	$550
0 days per week	5 days per week	$5	$250

9. **Avoid Adding New Debts**

   Cut up credit cards upon which you have no _____

   and close the accounts by calling your creditors.

10. **Develop a Debt-Management Plan**

    (The following steps are adapted from *Getting out of Debt, How Others Can Help You Get out of Debt and the Mississippi and Virginia Cooperative Extension.*)

    a. Find out how much you _____ and to whom.

    b. Decide how much you can pay back and when.

    c. Set up a plan for paying back your debts.

    d. Discuss your _____ with your creditors.

    e. Control spending by sticking with your debt-payment plan until debts are repaid.

11. Paying Back Your Debts

Debt payment can be done in several ways.

a. Pay each creditor equal amounts.

Debt	Amount Owed	Amount Required	Amount Able to Pay
Auto Loan	$1,145.39	$180	$60
Visa	680.30	35	60
Debt 1	525.00	170	60
Debt 2	755.00	190	60
Debt 3	275.00	25	60
	$3,380.69	$600	$300

b. Pay a larger portion to whom you owe the most and a smaller portion to whom you owe the least.

Debt	Amount Owed	Percent of Total	Amount Required	Amount Able to Pay
Auto Loan	$1,145.39	34%	$180	$102
Visa	680.30	20%	35	60
Debt 1	525.00	16%	170	48
Debt 2	755.00	22%	190	66
Debt 3	275.00	8%	25	24
	$3,380.69	100%	$600	$300

c. Figure what percent of the required amount you can afford to pay and pay that percentage to each creditor.

Debt	Amount Owed	Amount Required	Amount Able to Pay
Auto Loan	$1,145.39	$180 (x .50)	$90.00
Visa	680.30	35 (x .50)	17.50
Debt 1	525.00	170 (x .50)	85.00
Debt 2	755.00	190 (x .50)	95.00
Debt 3	275.00	25 (x .50)	12.50
	$3,380.69	$600	$300.00

12. Prioritizing Your Debt

When sufficient funds are not available to pay amounts required, consider

_____: i.e. mortgage first, credit cards second…

13. Communicate with Creditors

Creditors are _____ when you come up with a plan and even more so when you follow it – get them to agree with your plan.

14. Set a Financial Goal

Set a realistic goal for when you will be debt-free, i.e. 3 years.

15. Create a Spending Plan

a. Determine your _____ worth.

b. Track your cash flow.

c. Evaluate your monthly income sources.

d. Record your _____ expenses.

e. Keep a written account of your progress.

f. List all you owe first.

g. Create a _____ plan.

h. Assess the damage.

i. Pay the most expensive loan first.

j. Transfer your debts to a low-interest-rate credit card.

k. Cut up the high-rate cards you've paid off so you won't use them again.

l. Have a yard sale.

m. Keep a record of your _____ living expenses for a month.

n. Consider selling assets.

o. Increase your family income.

p. Borrow money as a last resort.

16. Determine & Reduce Your Time Goal

Because of compound interest, cutting the time you pay off a debt in half does not mean doubling the monthly payment, but rather slightly raising it.

17. Stay Focused on the Plan and Be Persistent.

18. Becoming Debt-Free

It is possible for most _____ to get out of debt within four years.

19. Simple – But Not Easy

When you encounter difficulties, don't run away from your creditors,

_____ with them. Consumer credit counseling

organizations also provide a helpful third party.

Like boot camp, becoming debt-free is not the end; rather, it's the beginning of a whole new adventure.

---

20. Your Decision to Change

Becoming debt-free can only happen if you are _____ committed.

21. Debt-Free Is Only the Beginning

22. The Picture of No Debt

The debt-free lifestyle looks like this.

a. You spend less than you earn.

b. You give.

c. You save.

d. You invest _____ and consistently.

e. Your financial decisions are purposeful.

f. You turn away from impulsive behavior.

g. You shun unsecured debt.

h.   You borrow cautiously.

i.   You _____ the unexpected.

j.   You scrutinize your purchases.

k.   You reach for your goals by following a _____ plan.

23. Handling Debt: The Courtroom

Handling debt by turning to the legal system is often costly and can involve serious financial consequences in the future.

24. Chapter 7 Bankruptcy

Filing bankruptcy allows one to be rid of most debt, but it also allows the court to liquidate their assets and pay off as much of the debt as possible.

25. Chapter 13 Wage-Earner's Plan

One can file Chapter 13 to _____ debts with the help of a court-ordered trustee who will garnish a percentage of wages earned to pay off debts over a period of time and help the filer manage their money.

26. Reward Yourself!

When you have come to the point of being debt-free, don't be afraid to treat yourself to an inexpensive _____. Just don't forget that after debt-recovery, the race to debt-prevention is on!

NOTES

STUDENT RESPONSE

Improvement Action Plan

What I need to change: _____

What? I define my goal as this achievable result. What will be my final outcome?

My answer: _____

_____

Why? This is why I need to accomplish my goal.

My answer: _____

_____

Who? Who will be involved in making me successful?

My answer: _____

_____

Where? Where will I get started? In what area will I begin?

My answer: _____

_____

How? How will I accomplish what I want to achieve? How will I measure my progress?

My answer: _____

_____

When? When will I begin working on achieving this goal?

My answer: _____

_____

Lesson Sixteen

MAKING LIFESTYLE CHANGES

"By what a man is overcome, by this he is enslaved."
II PETER 2:19

"Your servant... did this to change the present situation..."
II SAMUEL 14:20

"The plans of the diligent lead surely to advantage, but everyone who is hasty comes surely to poverty."
PROVERBS 21:5

"If you can't feed a hundred people, then feed just one."
MOTHER TERESA

"If you don't borrow money, you can't get into debt."

"It's not what you make; it's what you spend."

"Getting out of debt is an attitude before it is an action."

Lesson Sixteen

MAKING LIFESTYLE CHANGES

There are only five things you can do with money. Give it, save it, invest it, lend it, and spend it.

1. **Lifestyle Change Means Doing without the Non-Essentials**

2. **Lifestyle Change Means Paying with Cash**

3. **Lifestyle Change Means Committing to Godly Principles**

   "Blessings on all who reverence and trust the Lord— on all who obey Him! Their reward shall be prosperity and happiness." (Psalm 128:1,2)

   a. You must never keep it all.

   b. You must never _____ it all.

   c. God is your source.

   d. What you _____ is what you deserve.

4. **Lifestyle Change Means Learning Timely Principles**

5. **Lifestyle Change Means Decreasing Your Expenses**

   If Your Spending Is Out of Control…

   • As you pay off smaller debts, don't pay less each month on your overall debt, put that money towards another bill.

   • Ask for help and seek _____ about your situation.

   • Assess the damage.

- Avoid _____ or guaranteeing a loan for someone.
- Avoid further credit.

Debt is like cancer. It is not life-threatening at first because it involves only a cell or two, but it begins to grow and then it takes over.

- Avoid joint obligations with people who have _____ spending habits.
- Avoid large rent or house payments.
- Avoid _____ items (even if they're on sale).
- Barter your skills for someone else's skills.
- Be aware of the difference between wants and needs.
- Be aware of your spending habits.
- Be patient.
- Bring your lunch to work.
- Buy creative gifts as opposed to expensive gifts.
- Buy used items rather than new.
- Charge items only if you can _____ to pay for them now.
- Clip coupons and use them.
- Create a realistic budget and stick to it.
- Create a _____ plan.
- Credit Cards
    - i.   Pay more than the minimum monthly payment.
    - ii. Never use them to buy unbudgeted items.
    - iii. Pay off the balance in full each month.
    - iv. If you can't pay the whole monthly balance, destroy it!

    v.   Cut up cards for gas or department stores.

    vi.   Cut up high-rate cards you've paid off.

- Cut housing costs.
- Cut out _____ entertainment.
- Cut your cost of transportation.
- Deposit money in a _____ account regularly and leave it there.
- Determine your net worth.
- Develop a balanced budget that allows creditors to receive as much as possible.
- Develop a strategy.
- Do your own chores and repairs.
- Don't be so quick to pay down your mortgage.
- Don't expect instant miracles.
- Don't go broke on "good buys".

   "By what a man is overcome, by this he is enslaved." (II Peter 2:19)

- Don't make _____ investments.
- Drive your car an extra year or two before getting a new one.
- Eat oatmeal – it's healthy and filling.
- Eat out less and at home more.
- Eating in: use or freeze everything you buy.
- Drink _____ instead of soda.
- Enjoy the city parks.
- Evaluate your monthly income sources.
- Expect the unexpected.
- Fast food: don't order value meals.
- Find _____ to spending money.
- For extra income, peddle your skills.
- Forget about buying now, paying later.
- Get at least three prices for the same item from different sources.
- Get in shape: ride your bicycle to work.

- Get _____ insurance.
- Get the most for your money.
- Gifts: buy them all year long and keep a gift box to avoid expensive last minute shopping.
- Give to _____ first by saving.
- Go shopping with a list and buy only those items.
- Grow your own garden.
- Improve your gas mileage.
- Impulse _____ is a form of the get-rich-quick mentality.

  "The plans of the diligent lead surely to advantage, but everyone who is hasty comes surely to poverty." (Proverbs 21:5)
- Increase your insurance _____ to lower your monthly payment.
- Inform your kids and spouse of financial plans.
- Keep a "get rid of it" box and empty it twice annually.
- Keep a _____ record and a spending plan.
- Listen carefully.
- Live within your means.
- Look around for _____ insurance rates.
- Maintain a one-item wish list and compare prices.
- Maintain an _____ cash fund.
- Make a plan to pay off your debts.
- Make a resolution that you will NOT overspend ever again.
- Make long-distance calls only if _____ and at off-peak times.
- Make only one trip to the grocery store each week.
- Make _____ for life after debt.
- Make your own coffee.
- Make your own gifts.
- Minimize your debt.
- Most debt is bad.
- Move in with your parents (but only if you are single).

- Never _____ to buy depreciating items.

- Never buy anything unless you have budgeted for it.

- Only borrow for a home or college (or a car with zero percent financing).

- Pare down your _____ bill — eat rice and beans.

- Pay only with cash (but save your receipts).

- Pay off the most expensive loan first.

- Pay yourself by saving after you have tithed.

- Plan for the future.

- Practice _____ control.

- Retail Stores: Make an offer on floor models.

- Ride public transportation.

- Save all extra money.

- Save on supplies.

- Seek _____ help to work your way out of debt.

- Sell the new vehicle and settle for good used reliable transportation.

- Shop at thrift clothing stores.

- Start retiring the debt now.

- Stay away from convenience stores.

- Stay healthy.

- Stay home.

- Stay out of malls.

- Stop _____ debt.

- Stop spending!

- Subtract credit card purchases in your _____ register.

- Take advantage of free programs.

- There are no magic rules that solve financial troubles.

- Track your progress.

- Transfer your debts to a low-interest rate credit card.

- Try the Consumer Credit Counseling Service.

- Turn down the thermostat or air conditioning.

- Use _____, rebates and special promotions.

- Vacations: try a home exchange.

- Visit your local library.

- Wait at least _____ days to buy non-budgeted items.

- Wait _____ months and think it through before you purchase a "must have" item.

- When you pay off a car loan, keep investing that payment in mutual funds.

- You are never going to win the lottery so stop wasting your money.

NOTES

STUDENT RESPONSE

Improvement Action Plan

What I need to change: _____

What? I define my goal as this achievable result. What will be my final outcome?

My answer: _____

_____

Why? This is why I need to accomplish my goal.

My answer: _____

_____

Who? Who will be involved in making me successful?

My answer: _____

_____

Where? Where will I get started? In what area will I begin?

My answer: _____

_____

How? How will I accomplish what I want to achieve? How will I measure my progress?

My answer: _____

_____

When? When will I begin working on achieving this goal?

My answer: _____

_____

Lesson Seventeen

AREAS OF FINANCIAL VULNERABILITY

"By wisdom, a house is built and through understanding, it is established."
PROVERBS 24:3

"If something seems too good to be true, it probably is."

"A bank is a place where they lend you an umbrella in fair weather and ask for it back when it begins to rain."
ROBERT FROST

"When wealth is lost, nothing is lost; when health is lost, something is lost; when character is lost, all is lost."
BILLY GRAHAM

Lesson Seventeen

AREAS OF FINANCIAL VULNERABILITY

1. **The Vulnerability in Co-Signing**

    a. You are _____ the money.

    b. You are loaning the money.

    c. You are hoping your friend or relative will pay back the loan.

There is always someone willing to separate you from your money!

---

2. **The Vulnerability of Credit Scams**

    Strategies to _____ that you are the only one using your credit cards:

    a. Don't give your social security number to anyone except a brokerage, bank or employer.

    b. Destroy documents with _____ information before you throw them out.

    c. Demand that your credit card company stop selling your personal information (and don't give it away yourself by filling out surveys or sweepstakes entries).

    d. Contact the three credit bureaus and request that they put a "_____ alert" on your file.

3. **The Vulnerability of Get-Rich Schemes**

    a. Extended Warranties

    b. Credit Checks

c. Debt Consolidation

d. Too _____ to Be True

e. Other Money Pits

Ask questions, check the answers and consider all the facts before making that purchase or investing those hard-earned dollars.

NOTES

STUDENT RESPONSE

Improvement Action Plan

What I need to change: _____

What? I define my goal as this achievable result. What will be my final outcome?

My answer: _____

_____

Why? This is why I need to accomplish my goal.

My answer: _____

_____

Who? Who will be involved in making me successful?

My answer: _____

_____

Where? Where will I get started? In what area will I begin?

My answer: _____

_____

How? How will I accomplish what I want to achieve? How will I measure my progress?

My answer: _____

_____

When? When will I begin working on achieving this goal?

My answer: _____

_____

Lesson
Eighteen

INVESTING FOR
YOUR FUTURE

"He who works his land will have abundant food, but he who chases fantasies lacks judgement."
PROVERBS 12:11

"Steady plodding brings prosperity; hasty speculation brings poverty."
PROVERBS 21:5 (TLB)

"Our callings are not simply secular means of making money or a living, but are God's means of utilizing our gifts and interests to His glory."
A PARAPHRASE OF MARTIN LUTHER

Lesson Eighteen

INVESTING FOR YOUR FUTURE

1. Be Informed about Your Investment Risk

    a. Liquidity Risk

    b. Inflation Risk

    c. Economic Risk

    d. Interest Rate Risk

    e. Market Risk

    f. Company Risk

    g. Specific Risk

2. Know How to Minimize Your Investment Risk

    a. Diversification across Types of Securities

    b. Diversification across _____ Horizons

    c. Diversification across Industries

    d. Diversification among Different Companies

3. Steps to Investing Disaster

    a. The Foolishness of Failing to Set Goals

    b. The Foolishness of Giving up All Decisions to an Advisor

    c. The Foolishness of Failing to Find a Sensible Investment Strategy

    d. The Foolishness of Failing to Understand Risk and _____ Adequately

    e. The Foolishness of Trying to Time the Stock Market

    f. The _____ of Driving Your Investment Strategy with Taxes

        Divide the tax-exempt yield you are considering (i.e. 7 percent) by 1 less your tax bracket. (i.e. If you fall into the 28% federal tax bracket, this number would be $1 - 0.28 = 0.72$.) You would need to earn more than this number (i.e. 7 divided by 0.72 = 9.72 %) on a taxable investment to beat the return on a tax-exempt investment.

g. The Foolishness of Aggressively Seeking the _____ Yield

h. The Foolishness of Relying on Past Performance only for Investment Choices

i. The Foolishness of Underestimating the Effect of Commissions

j. The Foolishness of Failure to Keep _____ Tax Records

k. The Foolishness of Not Setting Aside Adequate Cash for Emergencies

l. The Foolishness of Underestimating Your Retirement Obligations

Plan to live until you are 90 and recognize that even moderate inflation of 5% annually can make your $1000 a month only worth what $277 is today.

m. The Foolishness of Sweating the _____ Stuff

If you are worried that another bank offers a quarter of an interest point more than yours does, don't be – you would only earn $2.50 annually per $1000 (upon which you must still pay taxes).

4. **Steps to Investing Success**

a. Establish investment objectives and _____ with them.

b. Invest for the long term.

c. Stay invested.

Generally, your money will double in the number of years equaled by the assumed interest rate divided into 72. (i.e. An investment at 7.5 percent will double in nine and a half years.)

d. Practice dollar-cost averaging.

By investing the same amount of money at _____ intervals, you will purchase fewer shares at high prices and more shares at lower prices, thus avoiding the guesswork involved in timing market ups and downs.

e. How does dollar-cost averaging work?

f. An Old Proverb

An old proverb says, "Steady plodding brings prosperity; hasty speculation brings poverty." (Proverbs 21:5, TLB)

5. Principles of Investing in Mutual Funds

a. The Principle of Seeking Out _____ Funds

   i.   Avoid stock funds with annual expenses that total more than 1.5% of the invested assets.

   ii. With international funds, this should be 2% or less.

   iii. With bond funds, insist on expenses below 1%.

b. The Principle of Dollar-Cost Averaging

c. The Principle of Building a _____ and Diversified Portfolio

d. The Principle of Understanding Market Indexes

   i.   S&P Composite Index

   ii.   Dow Jones Industrial Average

   iii. NYSE Composite Index

   iv.   Amex Market Value Index

   v.   NASDAQ Composite Index

   vi.   Russell 1000, 2000, 3000

   vii. Wilshire 5000

   viii. S&P Midcap 400

6. Online Educational Courses

- schwab.com
- kiplinger.com
- finance.yahoo.com
- smartmoney.com
- businessweek.com
- money.cnn.com
- fortune.com
- bloomberg.com
- investing.rutgers.edu
- morningstar.com
- quicken.com
- siebertnet.com
- moneycentral.msn.com
- flagship.vanguard.com
- fidelity.com
- standardandpoors.com

7. **Alternatives for Your Investment Consideration**

   a. Investment in Cash

   b. Investment in Bonds

   c. Investment in _____ Securities

   d. Treasury Notes And Bonds

   e. Zero Coupon Bonds

   f. Investment in Agency Securities

   g. Investment in Corporate Bonds

   h. Investment in _____ Bonds

   i. Investment in Common Stocks

   j. Investment in Money Market Funds

   k. Investment in Bond Mutual Funds

       i.   U.S. Government Bond Funds

       ii.   Mortgage-Backed _____ Funds

       iii.   Corporate Bond Funds

       iv.   Municipal Bond Funds

       v.   Current income

       vi.   Diversification

       vii. Stability

       viii. Professional management

       ix.   Liquidity

       x.   Convenience

       xi.   Tax consequences

       xii. Income fluctuation

   l. Investment in _____ Mutual Funds

       i.   Growth Funds

       ii.   Value Funds

       iii.   Blend Funds

       iv.   Small-Cap

       v.   Mid-Cap

       vi.   Large-Cap

m. Investment in Balanced Mutual Funds

The greatest benefit for the investor is that of diversification.

8. **Portfolio Strategy**

a. Risk Level I: _____ of Capital

    i.   20% Money Market Funds

    ii.   20% High Quality Bonds

    iii.   40% U.S. Treasury Bonds

    iv.   10% Growth and Income Funds

    v.   10% Growth Funds

b. Risk Level II: _____ Growth & Income

    i.   5% Money Market Funds

    ii.   20% U.S. Treasury Bonds

    iii.   40% Income Funds

    iv.   25% Growth and Income Funds

    v.   10% Growth Funds

c. Risk Level III: _____ Growth

    i.   10% Money Market Funds

    ii.   30% Growth and Income Funds

    iii.   30% Aggressive Growth Funds

    iv.   30% Income Funds

NOTES

STUDENT RESPONSE

Improvement Action Plan

What I need to change: _____

What? I define my goal as this achievable result. What will be my final outcome?

My answer: _____

_____

Why? This is why I need to accomplish my goal.

My answer: _____

_____

Who? Who will be involved in making me successful?

My answer: _____

_____

Where? Where will I get started? In what area will I begin?

My answer: _____

_____

How? How will I accomplish what I want to achieve? How will I measure my progress?

My answer: _____

_____

When? When will I begin working on achieving this goal?

My answer: _____

_____

Lesson Nineteen

PLANNING FOR RETIREMENT

"Then the LORD answered me and said: 'Write the vision and make it plain on tablets, that he may run who reads it."
HABAKKUK 2:2 (NKJV)

"Age-based retirement arbitrarily severs productive persons from their livelihood, squanders their talents, scars their health, strains an already overburdened Social Security system, and drives many elderly people into poverty and despair. Ageism is as odious as racism and sexism."
NORMAN VINCENT PEALE

"Preparation for old age should begin not later than one's teens. A life which is empty of purpose until 65 will not suddenly become filled on retirement."
DWIGHT L. MOODY

Lesson Nineteen

PLANNING FOR RETIREMENT

1. **Home Ownership**

   a. Home ownership is the first step toward a secure _____ future.

   b. Buying a home is more expensive than the first-time homebuyer can imagine.

   c. The greatest difficulty is _____ the necessary sum to cover the down payment and closing costs.

   d. Some lenders require a 10-20% down payment and closing costs can be 5% or more of the total purchase price, but are usually between 1-4%.

   e. Regularly saving and _____ those savings make owning your own home possible.

There is no secret to saving. It's really just a matter of living beneath your means.

---

2. **Saving for the First House**

   a. The short-term _____ of foregoing pleasant, but unnecessary, luxuries is worth the long-term benefits of owning a home.

   b. When you get paid, set aside savings first.

   c. Conservatively invest your _____ so it will earn you money.

   d. US government securities, CDs, zero coupon treasury bonds and low-risk mutual equity funds should be considered.

e. Mutual funds are recommendable.

f. Real estate is a _____ investment because, while your home increases in value, your mortgage payment does not.

g. Home ownership involves certain tax advantages.

h. By the time you want to retire, you can _____ your home at low or no cost or sell and buy a smaller home at no cost.

i. Rent payments only increase, never decrease.

3. **Strategies for Retirement Planning**

a. Know your _____ needs.

b. Know your future financial needs.

c. Know your housing needs.

d. Know your _____ needs.

e. Learn about your employer's pension or profit-sharing plan.

f. Contribute to a tax-sheltered savings plan.

g. Find out about your social security benefits.

h. Put money into an IRA – individual retirement account.

i. Protect your savings.

j. Follow basic investment principles.

k. Remember the rule of 72.

To discover when your _____ will double, divide 72 by the annual compound interest rate you expect to earn. If the rate is 7.2%, it will take 10 years to double your money.

l. Ask questions.

4. **Vehicles for Growing Your Retirement Savings**

a. Buy a home, contribute to an IRA and a deferred income plan such as a 401(k).

b. Do your own _____ because CPAs, financial planners and bankers are trying to sell you something.

5. Never Too Early, Never Too Late

    a. Start saving for retirement as soon as possible.

    b. The power of compound interest takes a little bit early on and makes it worth more than a lot invested later in life.

    c. Save _____ amounts on a weekly or monthly basis and it will turn into a lot bigger amount.

    d. It's never too late to start saving and if you start later in life, put away as much as you possibly can.

No one actively plans to fail in providing for a comfortable old age. They simply fail to plan.

---

6. Failing to Plan

    a. Be _____ for inflation, a sometimes down economy and the possibility of corporate fraud.

    b. Conserve not just principal, but purchasing power – the difference between earned interest and what inflation will take away.

7. Living on Less or Living on More

    a. It is a _____ that life will be cheaper when you are retired.

    b. In addition to higher medical, food, fuel, clothing, transportation and insurance costs, taxes will likely increase.

8. Social Security Benefits

    a. Social security will likely not be able to _____ very much security for those now 40 or younger.

    b. Family sizes also do not always decrease upon retirement.

    c. Prepare your _____ as best you can to live independently.

9. Living for the Moment

Live for the moment with 90% of your disposable income and save 10% for retirement.

10. How Much Do I Need?

a. Most financial planners feel that you need 60-90% of the _____ earned at the time of retirement.

b. Consider planning for extra expenses such as travel and medical.

11. The Inflation Concern

a. If you earn 7% on your _____, remember that 4% inflation reduces your purchasing power to 3%.

b. Your after-tax return on savings and investments should exceed inflation.

c. Divide the current inflation rate by 100 less your tax bracket. The percentage earned on your investment must exceed this number for your retirement savings to grow.

d. Social security can be drawn upon at 62, but the _____ is reduced. The longer you wait, the more beneficial.

12. How Will My Retirement Be Funded?

a. Request an _____ of your expected annual pension from your employee benefits department.

b. Frequent job changes can seriously impact retirement benefits.

13. Retirement Investment Products

a. Tax-Advantaged Retirement Products

b. Employer-Sponsored Retirement Plans

c. Cash Equivalents / Money Markets

d. Income Investments

e. Growth and _____ Investments

f. Growth Investments

g. Annuities

h. Mutual Funds

NOTES

STUDENT RESPONSE

Improvement Action Plan

What I need to change: _____

What? I define my goal as this achievable result. What will be my final outcome?

My answer: _____

_____

Why? This is why I need to accomplish my goal.

My answer: _____

_____

Who? Who will be involved in making me successful?

My answer: _____

_____

Where? Where will I get started? In what area will I begin?

My answer: _____

_____

How? How will I accomplish what I want to achieve? How will I measure my progress?

My answer: _____

_____

When? When will I begin working on achieving this goal?

My answer: _____

_____

Lesson Twenty

PREPARING FOR THE UNEXPECTED

"Go and make further preparation..."
I Samuel 23:22

"Spectacular achievement is always preceded by spectacular preparation."
ROBERT H. SCHULLER

Lesson Twenty

Preparing for the Unexpected

1. Natural Disasters

    a. Inventory your belongings.

    b. Use a _____ tape.

    c. Record make, model and serial numbers.

2. Loss of Employment

The possibility of losing one's job should be _____ enough to live free of debt.

3. Saving for Emergencies

    a. Three to six months' living expenses should be kept in safe, liquid cash investments for emergencies.

    b. Some _____ to Save For:

        i.   Travel expenses to family or relatives in case of illness or death

        ii.   Deductibles or co-payments on _____ expenses

        iii.   Auto insurance deductibles and temporary auto replacement, in case of an accident

        iv.   Auto repairs

        v.   Travel and gift expenses for _____ of family and friends

        vi.   Replacement of appliances that could break down

    c. Plan for these emergencies when you make your budget each year.

    d. Keep Your Emergency Fund in…

        i.   A savings account

        ii.   Bank money market deposit accounts

        iii.   Certificates of deposit (CDs)

iv.   Money market funds

4. Automatic Savings

a. If you are starting with no emergency fund, budget to pay _____ toward this.

b. Have it automatically deducted from your paycheck and put in a money market fund.

c. Whenever you get a _____, increase your savings by that amount.

5. Keeping Track of Important Papers

a. Your Will

b. Your Personal Papers

c. Your Advisors

d. Your Debts

e. Your Insurance

f. Your Savings and _____ Records

g. Your Safe-Deposit Box

6. Reviewing Your Insurance

a. Renters and Homeowners Insurance

b. Umbrella Insurance

c. Disability Insurance

d. Life Insurance

e. Auto Insurance

7. Proactively Prepared

While no one can _____ every situation, it is good to prepare responsibly as outlined above, and then to trust God.

NOTES

STUDENT RESPONSE

Improvement Action Plan

What I need to change: _____

What? I define my goal as this achievable result. What will be my final outcome?

My answer: _____

_____

Why? This is why I need to accomplish my goal.

My answer: _____

_____

Who? Who will be involved in making me successful?

My answer: _____

_____

Where? Where will I get started? In what area will I begin?

My answer: _____

_____

How? How will I accomplish what I want to achieve? How will I measure my progress?

My answer: _____

_____

When? When will I begin working on achieving this goal?

My answer: _____

_____

Answer Key

Lesson 1
1.a principles
2. anticipate
3.a. guiding
3.c. provider
4.a. contentment
4.c. opportunity
5.a. harm
5.c. human
6.b. morals
7.a. rob
7.c. honor
8.a. profit
8.c. clean
9.a. pre-occupied
9.c. tool
9.e. eternally
10.b. action
11. economy
12.a. little
13.a. possessing
13.b. riches
14.a. goods
14.b. invest
15.a. God
15.c. Desire
16.a. owner
16.c. eternal

Lesson 2
1.b. Water
2.a. increase
2.c. enriches
3.a. obligation
3.c. wealth
4.a. plant
4.c. always
4.e. reap
4.g. harvest
5.a. owns
5.b. Money
5.b.ii) accountability

5.b.iv) exposed
5.b.vi) blessing
5.b.viii) actions
5.c.ii) further
5.c.iii) everything
5.d.ii) priorities
5.d.iv) trigger

Lesson 3
1. give
3. nothing
4. ability
5. belong
6. source
7. abundant
8. important
9.a. stewards
9.c. tithed
9.e. tithe
11. tithed
14. seed
16. generosity

Lesson 4
1. cheerfully
3. (Bullets)
- owns
- proactive
- plenty
- advanced
- temporary
- systematic
- learning
- sacrificial
- faithfulness
- working
- refreshing
- understanding
- contentment
- hope
- guarding

- blessing
- financial
- full
- trusting
- right
- providing
- diligence
- enjoying
- freedom

Lesson 5
1.a. scriptural
1.b. possessions
3. overseeing
4. responsibility
6. complete
7. entire
9. everything
11. obey
13. manage
19. exercise
23. disciplined
25.a. laziness
25.c. gift

Lesson 6
1.a. wisely
1.c. investing
2.a. invest
3. important
4. purpose
5. account
6.c. regular
7. control
9. communicate
10.a.i) participation
10.b.i) share
10.c. Ready
11.a. Mean
11.d. Thinks
11.f. Said

Lesson 6 (continued)
12.b. objective
13.b. main
14.a. evaluation
14.c. attention
15.a. uncomfortable
16.a. common
17.b. positive
18. contract
19.a. reception
20.a. negative
21. communication

Lesson 7
1.a. understand
1.d. expenditures
2. judgement
3.b. choice
3.c. attitude
3.d.i. fulfillment
4.a. alternative
4.c.ii. managing
4.c.iii. decision
5.a. outcome
5.c. careful
6.a. mistakes
6.c. experience
6.e. Review

Lesson 8
1. satisfaction
2. recognizing
4. define
6. evaluate

Lesson 9
1. objectives
5. diligent
6. constantly
7.b. target
7.d. timeline
9. potential
10b. determination
16.c. Structure
16.f. Habit
17.b. Financial

18.b. right
18.e. build
18.h. prepares
19.c. standards
19.e. detailed
21.a. planning
21.b. developing
22.b. Ideas
23.g. Work
24.a. measurements
25.e. Updating

Lesson 10
1.a. account
1.c. discipline
2.a. expenses
2.b.i. picture
2.b.iii. fixed
2.b.v. daily
2.d.i. categories
2.d.iii. discretionary
2.g.i. spending
2.g.ii. mathematical
2.g.iv. framework

Lesson 11
1.a. free
1.c. enhance
2. (Bullets)
• tool
• opens
• keep
• team
• balance
• expenses
• goals
• realistically
• temptations
• gives
• advantage

Lesson 12
1.b. control
2.c. analyze
3.worksheet
4.b. save

4.f. impulse
4.k. interest-bearing
4.o. balance
4.r. budget
5.a. promptly
5.d. two
5.g. record
5.i. remember
6.c. Budget
6.g. Debt
6.l. Thinking

Lesson 13
1.b. long-range
1.f. increases
2.c. stumbling
3.b. Mutual
4.c. credit
4.h. retirement
4.l. spending
4.n.i. afford
4.o. doing
4.o.iv. lunch
4.o.vii. appreciate
4.o.xi. recreation
4.o.xiii. free
4.p. personal
4.r. Compound

Lesson 14
1. reveal
1.a. debt
1.c. Right
1.d. Self-controlled
1.e. Problem
1.f. Bondage
1.h. Borrowing
1.l. Impending
1.o. Credit
1.r. extension
1.w. Spotless
2.e. information
3.a. accounts
3.e. delinquent
3.h. fraudulent
4.f. Range

Lesson 14 (continued)
5.b. balances
8.a. Rebuild
8.d. mistakes
9.a.ii consolidate

Lesson 15
1. expenses
3. essential
4. habits
6. heroism
8. small
9. balance
10.a. owe
10.d. plan
12. prioritizing
13. impressed
15.a. net
15.d. monthly
15.g. payoff
15.m. current
18. families
19. communicate
20. totally
22.d. confidently
22.i. anticipate
22.k. specific
25. repay
26. reward

Lesson 16
3.b. spend
3.d. receive
5. (bullets)
- advice
- cosigning
- questionable
- unnecessary
- afford
- spending
- expensive
- savings
- high-risk
- water
- alternatives
- medical

- yourself
- buying
- deductibles
- spending
- better
- emergency
- necessary
- plans
- borrow
- grocery
- utility
- professional
- incurring
- checkbook
- coupons
- ten
- six

Lesson 17
1.a. borrowing
1. ensure
2.b. personal
2.e. "fraud"
3.d. Good

Lesson 18
2.b. Time
3.d. Diversify
3.f. Foolishness
3.g. Highest
3.j. Accurate
3.m. Small
4.a. stick
4.d. regular
5.a. Low-cost
5.c. Well-balanced
7.c. Treasury
7.h. Municipal
7.k.ii. Securities
7.l. Stock
8.a. Preservation
8.b. Conservative
8.c. Aggressive

Lesson 19
1.a. retirement
1.c. accumulating
1.e. investing
2.a. sacrifice
2.c. savings
2.f. solid
2.h. enjoy
3.a. retirement
3.d. health
3.k. investment
4.b. research
5.c. small
6.a. prepared
7.a. misconception
8.a. provide
8.c. children
10.a. income
11.a. investments
11.d. benefit
12.a. estimate
13.e. Income

Lesson 20
1.b. video
2. incentive
3.b. Emergencies
3.b.ii. medical
3.b.v.weddings
4.a. monthly
4.c. raise
5.f. Investment
7. foresee

Additional Equipping Resources by
Frank Damazio & Rich Brott

Biblical Principles for Becoming Debt Free!
Rescue Your Life & Liberate Your Future

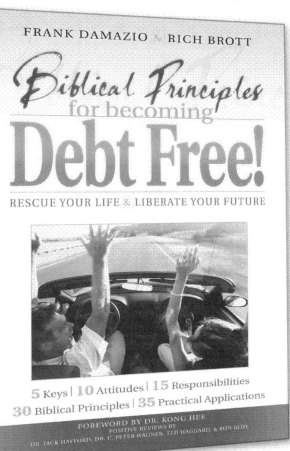

Dr. Jack W. Hayford
Chancellor, The King's College & Seminary

"There is a message of deliverance as well as a mandate to discipled living here–a balance I pray will bless multitudes."

Dr. C. Peter Wagner
Chancellor, Wagner Leadership Institute

"*Biblical Principles for Becoming Debt Free!* is your practical and exciting guidebook for making this happen!"

Ron Blue
President, Christian Financial Professionals Network

"It is a privilege for me to highly recommend this book. I want to encourage you to take to heart what God has to say about living your life with the financial freedom that comes from being debt-free."

Equip yourself with the 5 keys, 10 attitudes, 15 responsibilities, 30 attitudes, and 35 practical applications of acheiving financial freedom and fulfillment. Receive biblical teaching that will set a solid foundation on which to build a practical framework for a liberated financial future.

Complementary study materials...

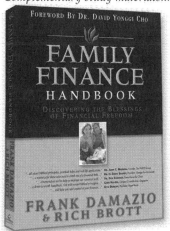

Family Finance Handbook

Paperback
7.5" x 10"
288 pages
ISBN 0-914936-60-3

$16.⁹⁹

$16.⁹⁹

Paperback, 7.5" x 10", 320 pages
ISBN 1-886849-85-4

CITY BIBLE
PUBLISHING

web: www.CityBiblePublishing.com
email: order@citybiblepublishing.com
phone: 1-800-777-6057